THE LANDLORD'S SURVIVAL GUIDE

HOW TO SUCCESSFULLY MANAGE RENTAL PROPERTY
AS A NEW OR PART-TIME REAL ESTATE INVESTOR

JEFFREY TAYLOR
"MR. LANDLORD"

— FRAUdulent Conveyance

KAPLAN) PUBLISHING

This publication is designed to provide accurate and authoritative information in regard to the subject matter covered. It is sold with the understanding that the publisher is not engaged in rendering legal, accounting, or other professional service. If legal advice or other expert assistance is required, the services of a competent professional person should be sought.

President, Dearborn Publishing: Roy Lipner
Vice President and Publisher: Maureen McMahon
Senior Acquisitions Editor: Victoria Smith
Production Editor: Karen Goodfriend
Creative Director: Lucy Jenkins
Cover Design: Gail Chandler
Typesetter: the dotted i

Published by Kaplan Publishing
a division of Kaplan, Inc.

Printed in the United States of America

07 08   10 9 8 7 6 5 4

Library of Congress Cataloging-in-Publication Data

Taylor, Jeffrey, 1958–
    The landlord's survival guide for the new and part-time real estate investor / Jeffrey Taylor.
        p.   cm.
    Includes index.
    ISBN-13: 978-1-4195-3569-7
    ISBN-10: 1-4195-3569-2
1. Real estate management. 2. Rental housing—Management. 3. Landlord and tenant. I. Title.
    HD1394.T3955 2006
    333.5′4—dc22   2006000200

PRAISE FOR *THE LANDLORD'S SURVIVAL GUIDE*

*"In The Landlord's Survival Guide, Jeff Taylor shares fresh ideas and fresh
perspectives that will help make any landlord more productive."*
**LEIGH ROBINSON, AUTHOR OF LANDLORDING: A HANDY MANUAL FOR SCRUPULOUS LANDLORDS AND
LANDLADIES**

*"I personally use Jeffrey Taylor's strategies with my rental properties and it results
in better residents, more cash flow, and less headaches. I would highly
recommend that every landlord buy his book."*
ATTORNEY WILLIAM BRONCHICK, AUTHOR OF THE BEST SELLING BOOK FLIPPING PROPERTIES

*"If everyone owning real estate were forced to read Jeffrey's book there would be a
lot more multimillionaires and more tenants happy with their landlords.
It's a must read for serious real estate investors."*
**RON LEGRAND, AUTHOR OF THE BUSINESSWEEK BEST-SELLER HOW TO BE A QUICK TURN REAL
ESTATE MILLIONAIRE**

*"The Landlord's Survival Guide will help you make more money and save you a lot of
headaches in managing property. There are a ton of great ideas that really work.
Read this book and do what it says . . . it works!"*
ROBERT SHEMIN, AUTHOR OF SECRETS OF A MILLIONAIRE REAL ESTATE INVESTOR

*"Not only is The Landlord's Survival Guide great for new and part-time real estate investors, it
is extremely helpful for new property managers who are starting out managing other people's
property or for the long time property manager wanting new tips and a great reference guide."*
**MELISSA PRANDI, MPM, AUTHOR OF THE UNOFFICIAL GUIDE TO MANAGING RENTAL PROPERTY AND
PAST PRESIDENT OF THE NATIONAL ASSOCIATION OF RESIDENTIAL PROPERTY MANAGERS**

*"Jeffrey's creative people management techniques are worth BIG money
to all landlords–from beginners to old salts alike."*
JAY DECIMA, AUTHOR OF START SMALL, PROFIT BIG IN REAL ESTATE

*"Mr. Landlord's ideas have increased the profits from my apartments every time I've
applied them! If you want bigger cash flows and smaller hassles, read this book!"*
PETER CONTI - CO AUTHOR OF INVESTING IN REAL ESTATE WITHOUT CASH OR CREDIT

*"The vast majority of my real estate association members are part-time real estate investors
and landlords. I've invited Jeffrey to speak to our association annually for over 10 years
because he is the real deal and members appreciate his practical and proven advice that
generates results. I'd encourage every real estate association to get enough copies of Jeffrey's
Survival Guide to offer to all their members and as a gift for all new and renewing members."*
DAN FALLER, PRESIDENT OF THE APARTMENT OWNERS ASSOCIATION OF CALIFORNIA

DEDICATION

I dedicate this book to Dot Taylor, my business partner, best friend, and wife of nearly 25 years, for her love, support, business acumen, savviness, and patience—both working with me and showing me how to enjoy the fruits of our efforts.

Together we have built a real estate investing and consulting business that now spans the globe. She has assisted, taught, and traveled with me to reach subscribers in more than a dozen countries. When we married, I'm sure she, like me, wasn't aware that one day we'd be traveling and teaching in such places as Australia or New Zealand. To Dot, I will be forever grateful.

And to our sons, Jeffrey and Justin. I hope we've set an example and legacy of faith and entrepreneurship that inspires them to always seek the unlimited options available to them. My heart is touched when I see excitement in the eyes of one son who collects coins from the laundry machines at a rental building because I know a flame has been ignited. We're amazed when we watch our other son use computer skills to design programs that go beyond our imaginations and add to our real estate conferences and cruises. Whether their fire continues to burn brightly in real estate, law, or video game programming, time will only tell. My wife and I are blessed to know that we played a part in encouraging our sons to always strive (though not to be consumed by the fire) to be lights of excellence in whatever they do.

C o n t e n t s

I would like to acknowledge the following individuals who have been a part of our success team over the years offering assistance, inspiration, and support that has allowed me to write this guide: Al Aiello, Janis Baker, Paul Bauer, William Bronchick, John Burley, Jay DeCima, Rick Degelsmith, Dan Faller, Jane Garvey, Mary Good, Nick Koon, Ron LeGrand, Al Lowry, Dr. B. Courtney McBath, Melissa Prandi, Leigh Robinson, Robert Shemin, Ruby and Ervin Taylor (nothing possible without my loving mom and dad), and Wright Thurston. I also wish to express my appreciation to numerous authors, trainers, and business associates I've had the privilege to work with—especially the hundreds of real estate association leaders who have welcomed me into their meetings and allowed me to share my unique management concepts with their members.

For editing this manuscript, special thanks to Barbara McNichol—a diligent and great team member to work with who kept me on track as best she could. Her work has definitely added to the clarity of the action steps presented in this guide.

I must give thanks to the hundreds of thousands of real estate investors who have subscribed and contributed to the *Mr. Landlord* newsletter and to the MrLandlord.com Web site. For the housing service you provide to millions and the challenges you face without thanks or recognition, I salute you!

And finally, the highest acknowledgment is to God be the Glory, The Landlord of all. I give Him thanks and praise for the assets, opportunities, and grace He has given and continues to give.

Jeffrey Taylor, respectfully and rightfully known as Mr. Landlord, has totally revolutionized the landlording business with his cutting-edge marketing ideas and dynamic cash flow programs.

I have read Jeffrey's first book, *The Landlord's Kit*, and subscribed to his newsletter, *Mr. Landlord*, since late 1980s. His books and newsletters are the best resources available in the country for real estate investors managing their property part-time. His moneymaking and moneysaving ideas are clearly explained and based on proven real-world experiences. I know this because—along with being a tax specialist, real estate instructor, and former real estate broker—I'm also a rental property owner. I have implemented Jeffrey's ideas and have greatly benefited from them. Just the one idea (among hundreds) of calling renters "3-Star Residents" instead of "tenants" is powerful unto itself.

I remember taking Jeffrey's advice on sending thank-you notes to good residents from time to time, just saying, "Thank you for being a great resident. —Albert Aiello, Assistant Manager." One of my residents was so appreciative that he ended up buying one of my properties. And notice how the note was signed with "Assistant Manager" after my name instead of "Owner"—a great Jeffrey Taylor tip on privacy to never let your residents know you are the owner.

Another strategy is to employ special "custom home" marketing packages to promote optional property upgrades (e.g., ceiling fans, microwaves, computers, TVs, etc.) as an additional source of income. Using this technique on one small multiunit property, I increased my annual cash flow by $6,500. And with a 10 percent capitalization rate, I also increased the value of my property by $65,000. Not bad for one cash flow idea among so many.

Not long ago, I met a real estate attorney who subscribes to Jeffery's cash flow strategies. Every two years, he replaces all of the computers and related equipment in his law offices, even though they're still working. He then leases the replaced computers to his residents for additional income using Jeffrey's super-size-it strategy.

Jeffrey makes landlording not only highly profitable, but fun! I could go on and on with Jeffrey's ingenious moneymaking ideas, but I'll conclude by saying that he's without a doubt the number one landlording coach in America, and *no one else* in the world deserves the title Mr. Landlord.

Sincerely,

Albert Aiello, CPA, MS Taxation, RE Investor, RE Broker, National Instructor

THE STEPS TO LONG-TERM WEALTH

WHAT THIS GUIDE WILL HELP YOU DO

This *Landlord's Survival Guide* is for real estate investors who want to profit from their rental properties and wish to, or only have time to, deal with them part-time. *You* have picked up this book because you now own one or two rental properties (or soon will) and want to make the most money possible without any headaches, or you have several properties and want greater success. Perhaps you've been managing properties awhile and feel burned out, frustrated, or overwhelmed. I've got good news!

This guide shows you a whole new way of managing properties that will remove frustrations, eliminate headaches, and have residents working *with* you instead of *against* you. It also shows you how to manage your properties in ways that free your mind and your time—enough so you can continue to expand your real estate wealth.

The guesswork has been removed. The core of this book is made up of clear action steps. This guide is not an overview or a textbook of management theories. It's an actual "playbook" that shows you how to win! When you need to fill a vacancy, just follow the steps. When you need more cash flow or need to collect money due you, just follow the steps. If you want to keep a resident longer, just follow the steps. You'll never have to wonder or figure out what to do to increase your management success. You'll simply pull out this guide and make it happen. And because I know different people sometimes like to take different approaches, at times, I'll share a couple of alternative steps you can take so you can choose the approach that works best for you.

After following the action-oriented steps in this guide, you'll watch your properties fill with ideal residents, watch your current residents stay longer, and watch your cash flow increase—without the headaches that typical landlords experience. More money with fewer worries—I guarantee it! That's how I define successfully managing rental property as a part-time real estate investor.

WHAT THIS GUIDE WILL NOT HELP YOU DO

Unlike most other "landlording" books, this guide is *not* intended to turn you into a typical landlord who cleans and paints properties on the weekend or repeatedly gets calls from residents at all hours to fix whatever's broken. Forget that! That's not how to enjoy managing your investments part-time and build wealth.

This guide encourages you to develop a success team to help you run your rental business. Most important, it reveals how to get your residents to play a major role on your success team. Its core focus is on how to select, communicate, and work with ideal residents. How? By giving them the right incentives so they willingly form long-term, mutually beneficial relationships with you.

People- (Not Property-) Centered Management

There's no need to be scared of landlording nightmares you've heard from other investors or experienced yourself. You can change that with a people-centered approach to rental property management. I've made a 24-year career of owning and managing all types of rental properties. Today, I show real estate investors throughout the world how to maximize their income part-time without the hassles typical landlords face—and have peace of mind as a result. In your hands, you hold information I've learned the hard way. It's information well worth paying thousands of dollars to know—information I wish I'd had when I first started.

The truth is you will pay less than $30 to learn what's in this valuable guide or you can learn through costly trial and error. I know that if you embrace the lessons within, you'll reach your real estate and financial goals a lot faster. And you'll do it without the headaches that overtake many investors—or scare them away altogether. Don't miss out on the greater rental property riches that come from holding on to properties over time.

Once you have the right mindset, a landlording success team in place to handle various aspects of your rental property business, and an understanding of key obligations and laws, you have taken the first three essential preparatory steps for survival. Then you can follow the next seven steps to overcome the key management challenges for every real estate investor that determine their level of rental property success. The seven action steps emphasized in this guide are:

1. How to fill vacancies with ideal residents
2. How to screen out "problem" residents
3. How to address potential problems before they occur
4. How to get your money from your residents
5. How to maximize your rental income
6. How to keep residents much longer than one year
7. How to end the rental relationship and continue making profits

The core of this guide goes into detail providing hundreds of step-by-step, practical, proven, innovative strategies to master management challenges. By using this guide over and over—repeating the steps with every property you own or control—you'll achieve maximum profits and cash flow success.

THREE
PREPARATORY STEPS

1

DEVELOP THE RIGHT MINDSET

*"You must run your rental business,
don't let the business run you.*
—ROBERT SHEMIN

Let me propose a few business principles that are key for you to develop the right mindset for survival—and success—in today's world.

After learning so much the hard way in my early years, I started using the principles that have greatly added to my success and the success of thousands of rental owners. Some say that real estate investing isn't for everybody—and that may be true. However, many don't succeed because they simply never develop the kind of mindset needed to work effectively with residents and management situations. Many burn out, get frustrated, and give up. Fear not! That doesn't have to happen to you! Adopt the right mindset and you'll realize more success as a real estate investor.

PROACTIVE BUSINESS MINDSET

Many landlords react to problems only when a need arises. That's because they haven't developed a system—a series of action steps and checklists to follow in key areas of their rental businesses. Most new and part-time investors see their rental property as something to deal with "on the side" for extra income, tax benefits, or wealth building.

Yes, real estate investing remains one of the best ways for the average Jack or Jill to build wealth part-time. But never assume that your rentals and your residents (even if you only have one or two) will keep producing positive results without having a proactive, systematic approach to managing them. If you take a *proactive* instead of a reactive management approach and follow the action steps outlined, you can meet your goals *and* manage your rentals in less time with far fewer hassles.

GOAL-DIRECTED MINDSET

Operating in a businesslike manner requires having goals or targets at which to shoot. Average landlords have no goals in mind; they adopt a "survival" mentality instead of a "success" mentality. When residents don't call with problems, they say, "Wow, no calls this month. It's been a great month." But you're not reading this to learn how to merely survive; you want to achieve outstanding results. You want to make the most headache-free income possible working the least amount of time.

Start by establishing goals in each key management area. For example, in the area of vacancies, I aim to fill a vacancy within 72 hours or at the most 7 days. Regarding cash flow, I aim to increase my net operating income a minimum of 10 percent a year. Regarding resident retention, I aim to have residents stay an average of 5 to 6 years. Regarding rent collection, I aim to collect *all* money due me. Regarding resident cooperation and satisfaction, I aim to have any resident who has violated a term in the rental agreement to correct the violation within 72 hours. I aim *not* to have repeat violators residing in my properties. And I aim to have residents each refer at least one other person to me—a person who wants to either rent a home or sell one. I encourage you, too, to adopt a goal-directed mindset.

After hearing some of my management goals at seminars, real estate investors ask: Wow, where do you find residents to stay in your property at least five years? Where do you find people who pay you on time every month? Where do you find residents who take care of your property correctly and follow your rules? Where do find residents who refer others to you? Where do you find residents willing to help you reach your goals?

Here's one of my biggest management "secrets": I don't find them; I *entice* them. I use systematic action steps from the first day I meet them and throughout the mutually beneficial rental relationship.

PEOPLE-CENTERED MINDSET

Through incentives, I entice applicants and residents to work within my management programs. First, I ask them about their current and future housing needs. I show them how the company I work for can meet those needs. I also tell applicants and regularly remind residents about different ways we reward their longevity and cooperation. (See Steps 4 through 10 for specific strategies from filling your vacancy to the end of the rental relationship—all part of my systematic way to getting residents to become cooperative members of your success team.)

You may ask, "Why do I need to entice my residents or seek to meet their needs? Either I have properties they want or I don't. They either follow my rules or get out." That mentality comes from the "old school" of property management. I want to create a new school for investors who've started within the past five years and for part-time investors who have landlorded for years in frustration and want more effective ways to manage their rentals.

I believe that success as a landlord is not about property management but about successfully applying good people management skills. That's why I propose a type of management that's not only proactive but people centered. It advocates building win-win relationships between you and your residents—all while helping you reach your management goals.

Conventional wisdom in this business often reflects an "it's my way or the highway" attitude. That means if prospective residents don't go along with the rules, landlords say "Next!" and move on to other options.

Understand that the newest generation of residents has grown up in an environment where businesses market their products by saying, "Have it your way!" That's why you can't manage your properties in a way that dictates your way or the highway. These two mindsets directly conflict!

By saying this, I don't suggest that you heed the whims of your residents or even bend whatever rules you establish. And while I believe in setting and enforcing certain rules, it's also critically important to develop a win-win relationship with residents so they believe they're winning along with you.

In addition to setting rules, you must also offer (and invite residents to participate in) different types of carefully designed programs that give them options and help you reach your goals. They may include different incentives such as choices of amenities or extras, choices of automatic payment, choices of rent payment due dates, choices of anniversary benefits and homebuyer plans, etc. This is how rental residents can have it their way.

Here's the best news. You'll discover that by having a people-centered mindset, you'll separate yourself from competitive rental properties. This attitude will help you attract residents willing to pay more, pay on time, stay longer, and be more cooperative with you.

I contend it's even more critical because of the competitive environment landlords face today. Your challenge calls for developing a solid reputation that allows positive word-of-mouth advertising to keep your business going. If your residents feel good about where they live, they tell others. They're also less likely to bother you about every little thing *if* they believe you're fair with them. Conversely, if you cultivate a me-against-them attitude, they'll take the first available opportunity to sue you. The message: Let your residents know you look forward to serving them, working with them, and rewarding them for being with you over the years.

Naturally, you have to start by attracting the right type of residents. More than 90 percent of the problems landlords deal with can be traced to selecting the wrong residents. Steps 4 and 5 offer key questions, strategies, and screening procedures to attract and identify qualified residents, plus ways to target your marketing efforts.

Note: I want to emphasize that even after careful screening and selection, no applicants show up declaring they plan to stay for the next five years. No residents start the relationship planning to pay you more money every year and pay you like clockwork. None show up volunteering to take great care of your property and cooperate with all your rental policies—even if problems occur that aren't their fault.

Your applicants will come to you just like the potential problem residents who show up at every landlord's door. What's the difference? Through small but systematic management practices and enticements, you can turn marginal-to-average residents into good residents, and turn good residents into great residents. They'll become part of your success team—and help you reach your goals.

TEAM MEMBER MINDSET

Make residents your business partners who play a vital role in your success. The average landlord doesn't regard residents as business partners, which I think is a mistake. But residents can make or break your success, so having an adversarial mindset toward them won't work.

Notice, I don't use the word *tenant*. In my mind and in the mind of renters themselves, the word *tenant* has connotations that don't gel with my management goals. I think of a tenant as someone who stays temporarily, who willingly only pays so much, and who only takes care of the property to a certain level.

Many landlords complain about how people aren't performing—they don't pay on time, they neglect the property, they skip out in the middle of the night. They act just like tenants! Even the word *tenant* sounds temporary—like someone with whom you don't have a long-term relationship. I think this term goes to the crux of the communication issue—what *you* expect of people and what *they* think you expect of them. I avoid saying tenants because I don't want people who rent my properties to act like average tenants!

So from day one, I call them "3-Star Residents" because I want them to think of themselves that way. Later, they become Future Homebuyers, which aligns with their dreams and my management goals. (You'll read about these programs in Steps 9 and 10.)

LIFETIME CUSTOMER MINDSET

When I see a prospective resident, I don't just see someone who may pay me $700 a month in rent. Instead, I look at the lifetime resident value of that customer. In fact, creating a lasting relationship could easily total more than $100,000 in income for me, per resident.

Here's how I calculate that $100,000 value. In the area of my properties, the average rental goes for $700 a month, which is $8,400 a year. My average resident stays with me five years. Starting at $700 a month and not even including a 5 percent annual increase, after five years, that totals $42,000. Where do I get the rest of the value? Two ways.

First, your current residents can become your best future customers. How? By assisting them with their current *and* future housing needs. Once you've established a good rental relationship, you could earn money on the back end by selling properties to them. You can offer to partially finance the sale and set up a powerful win-win situation. One of my goals is to receive mortgage payments from my residents after the rental relationship is over for at least five to ten more years. With just five years of $300 a month income from mortgage payments following the rental relationship, that's another $18,000 received. That total, added to the rental income of $42,000, makes for a sum of $60,000.

Second, with my free upgrade referral program, another goal is that sometime during their tenancy each of my residents refers at least one other person who rents from me. In essence, each person duplicates themselves. That doubles their lifetime value with each being worth $120,000. Even a $500-a-month rental resident (with annual rent increases over five years) can generate $100,000 over a lifetime. And if your property rents for closer to $1,000 monthly or higher, do the math. The lifetime resident value of each customer can climb to $200,000. Looking at things this way, you should never regard a resident in the old way.

CHALLENGE-PREPARED MINDSET

Even though you'll learn to get residents to work *with* you and not *against* you, challenges will still occur. Realize this: Yes, things sometimes go wrong. (Were you expecting me to say something more profound?) By the way, something going wrong isn't the same as having a perpetual rental headache, which happens because you don't expect something to happen and don't know how to deal with it.

Note: If you catch on to what I'm sharing, you won't have rental headaches as a real estate investor. For example, say a resident doesn't pay rent when it's due. (You'd be amazed how many landlords act shocked or get frustrated when this occurs—as though they thought it would never happen.) Here's the real problem: Most landlords don't prepare for how to reduce the chances of this occurring. Or they don't know what steps to take to cause positive results. They go through their day-to-day activities "hoping" common problems won't ever occur.

Too Much "Hoping"

When I started as a real estate investor, my hope factor was high. I did a lot of hoping. I used to run rental ads in the newspaper and hope people would call. If they called, I hoped they'd show up for the appointment. If they showed up, I hoped they'd like my place. If they liked it, I hoped they'd qualify.

Folks, that's too much hoping. And if all that hoping got me new residents, well, once they moved in, the hoping didn't stop there. I hoped they'd pay me (and on time). I hoped they wouldn't tear up the place; hoped they'd stay—hoped, hoped, hoped.

What makes matters worse? Becoming disappointed by these challenges and blaming residents for them. Why haven't they paid me? Why didn't they do that particular thing? Blah, blah, blah. Some landlords get fed up and get out of the game, or try to play it without doing the management side. What a shame! So much potential for long-term, massive wealth can be built from real estate by holding and managing properties well.

If you're properly prepared to deal with things that happen, you've already given yourself an entirely different mindset than the average real estate investor. The right mindset starts with never blaming your resident for your problems, even if you think you have good reason to feel that way. That will, indeed, delay you in your quest for success because you'll less likely seek ways of improving. I'll say it again: *Never blame your residents.*

Instead, have a mindset that responds to challenges by asking yourself, "What can I do differently to prevent that same problem from happening again? What proactive management practices can I put in place to increase the odds of reaching my management goals?"

Take the "hope" factor out of your business thinking. And be ready to take preplanned action steps when things don't go as expected. Reread this step and review it often. By embracing various principles of the right mindset—and by following the management practices and seven action steps in this guide—you'll manage your real estate more effectively than the average landlord and achieve better results.

2

IDENTIFY YOUR LANDLORDING SUCCESS TEAM

"You don't have to know how to do everything to be successful with real estate; you just need to know the right people to call for help."
—JEFFREY TAYLOR

Do *not* try to do everything yourself!

That is a common mistake I see with real estate investors who are the "independent" types. They buy a rental property and try to run everything related to its operation. As a result, they turn into the "typical" landlord and greatly limit their growth potential.

Typical landlords try to do all the maintenance on the property themselves. They prepare their own taxes and do their own bookkeeping to save money by not hiring others. But if Sam Walton were still alive, you wouldn't walk into Wal-Mart and see Sam stocking the shelves, cleaning up the spill in Aisle 5, checking you out at the cash register, preparing paperwork for the auditor, and bringing in shopping carts from the parking lot. Whether you run Wal-Mart or your own real estate investment business, doing all the work yourself is not how to "manage" a business. If you do, you'll feel chained to your properties doing what needs to be done and feel overwhelmed. You want to freely focus on building your real estate portfolio.

In this guide, I offer tips on dealing with issues that make the most difference in managing your properties: selecting and screening business partners (your residents), and training and managing *them* rather than managing properties. Face it. You can find qualified plumbers to fix a toilet and hire experts to handle taxes or lawsuits. But few individuals know how to attract and select ideal residents to fill vacancies quickly—or train and keep them for six years while creating a desire to cooperate with your policies and increasing your net operating income. The learning curve for becoming a master plumber, electrician, accountant, or attorney goes beyond what can be taught here. But I can teach you part-time management strategies and practices that will greatly increase your success, plus give you time to enjoy life.

It's best to identify competent individuals in different areas and hire them when needed. Yes, you'll have to pay for their expertise, but by hiring them, they'll save or make you more money than it costs to *not* hire them. That should be your criterion. Understanding this point has greatly helped me overcome my "frugal" landlording mentality.

Focus first on management practices so you can increase and maintain your rental revenue stream. Beyond that, focus on activities that can bring in even more revenue. Does it make sense to save $100 working all day to fix a plumbing problem when you could have located another property that would bring in a few hundred a month positive cash flow and tens of thousands in profit?

Having a team of competent individuals makes the difference between acquiring only one or two rentals and building a portfolio of dozens of properties. Who do you need to help you? Identify them and ask them to be ready to solve problems that arise. Just knowing who's on your success team relieves stress and keeps your mind clear to determine the best use of your time. That's how to enjoy life better as a part-time real estate investor.

FAMILY MEMBERS

Spouse. My spouse, Dot, made me realize the significance of bringing a spouse onto your success team. With her assistance, we purchased far more properties than I could have done alone. She trains real estate investors at our annual Landlord Cruise Conferences and Trainings. She warns them not to mistakenly or unknowingly have their absolute best player sitting on the bench instead of working with them. Even if only one person in the couple is actively involved, it helps if a spouse or partner knows *how* to support the active investor. Dot tells couples to make sure they *both* have goals—to determine what they hope to get from the profits generated. When I started investing, I had goals of simply buying more properties and having more cash flow. However, Dot had goals of moving into a nicer home, taking fun family vacations, and using money for special nonrental projects. When we started assigning a portion of the "profit" earned toward her goals, her motivation to assist in our real estate endeavors increased dramatically. We've been able to buy and control more properties because of her support, assistance, and encouragement. She even wrote a book on how real estate couples can work together without going insane.

Children. The idea of having goals for both spouses in a marriage should extend to all other members of the family. We have two sons, Jeffrey and Justin. From the fruits of our real estate efforts, each year we reward them with something they desire and enjoy—such as a trip to Florida and a three-day pass to an amusement park when they were young. As they grew older, they wanted a cabin of their own on our weeklong landlord cruises. These rewards became possible because of their assistance and support—and they fully understand that. During the year, they may have to sacrifice having their parents available. They appreciate that our family exchanges buying something that's immediately gratifying for delayed but greater returns in the future. Of course, having them physically assist with rental activities helps, too. I even suggest paying your children a "tax-deductible" salary for their help, which may give you tax advantages. Use the salaries you pay them to purchase things they need. Most likely, your children fall into an income bracket that requires them to pay no (or little) tax on money earned. Discuss details with your tax advisor, another member of your real estate success team.

TRUSTED ADVISORS

The more loyal resources you know on a first-name basis and the more business you do with them, the more success you will have. When you find competent business professionals, use their services and products over and over.

Many investors don't understand the absolute necessity of developing loyal, strong business relationships. Instead, some buy from whomever has the cheapest price or the closest location. That never builds loyalty. Sure, you might save a few bucks in the short term, but that's not a formula for long-term success. You want to call on dependable individuals as needed and get reliable, valuable service. Changing the people you work with is like rolling the dice: Each transaction increases your odds of facing inconsistent quality and higher costs in the long run.

As you identify members for your success team, use them often. Refer others to them. In exchange, they'll be more likely to give you "preferential" service and discounted prices. I think the preferential service is more valuable than discounts. Being able to call (on a first-name basis) a trusted attorney, accountant, banker, financial advisor, and reliable real estate agents, contractors, and storeowners to ask questions on short notice is priceless. I suggest establishing long-term relationships with professionals in the following positions immediately.

Attorney. Find a legal expert who will handle your real estate transactions and closings. Selecting someone familiar with your buying methods helps make closings go smoothly and prevents costly glitches that could jeopardize a deal. Especially when starting out, your attorney can counsel you on landlord-tenant laws, review your standard rental agreement, and perhaps assist with evictions. Your attorney can also help you with asset protection and estate planning. If you can't find an attorney who's an expert in all three areas, that's okay. It's wiser to hire several attorneys who specialize in different areas than have one "general" attorney.

Accountant. You can lose thousands of dollars by not taking advantage of the tax deductions to which real estate investors are entitled. Work with CPAs who own real estate themselves and stay on top of new tax laws related to real estate investors.

Contractors. Identify at least two general contractors who can handle almost any kind of maintenance repairs. To find dependable ones, I suggest seeking references from other investors or landlords. Any contractor hired should be licensed, bonded, and insured. When in the presence of contractors, learn maintenance "tricks of the trade." Contractors are often quick to share their experiences and mistakes. Also develop a list of specialized contractors (e.g., electrician, roofer, appliance repairperson, floor covering installer, plumber, heating technician, etc.). By establishing relationships ahead of time, you won't panic when an emergency occurs. You simply pick up the phone.

Insurance agent. First, consider working with the same agent who handles the insurance protection on your primary residence or home. If that's not possible, work with an agent who offers rental property insurance coverage. Your insurance coverage should protect you against fire, vandalism, lost rent, and liability. Having proper insurance is critical because it protects you against catastrophic financial claims. Because insurance costs vary, have an independent agent find you the best coverage for your money. Consider purchasing an umbrella insurance policy or blanket coverage to decrease your liability even more.

Real estate agent/broker. Agents help you find rentals to buy, assist you in selling property, and give you information on the value of comparable properties. Determine which type of properties are you most interested in (e.g., single family, small multifamily, or large apartment buildings) and select agents/brokers who specialize in the type of properties you want to buy.

Property manager. This person assists with management responsibilities. If you buy right, there should be enough built-in cash flow or profit to hire a manager to handle most management duties. I like hiring property management firms that draw from a proven group of reliable contractors. That way, I don't spend my energies and focus dealing with maintenance. Instead, I keep my mind free to generate more income. By the way, if you find property managers who are especially skillful in "people management" and already implement many of my management practices, get to know them. They may be willing to assist you as they see you as a potential future client.

Seek their counsel and possibly use their services, especially if you move away or decide you don't want to be involved in management at all. Good property managers are well worth their fees. Remember, when selecting managers, seek references and look for those with specialized management training, sometimes indicated by a designation behind their name. Don't hire just any real estate company; most only focus on buying and selling properties themselves. Look for companies that specialize in property management and belong to the National Association

Hiring Tips

When hiring property managers, follow these five tips:

1. Don't sign a long-term agreement (beyond a year).
2. Have them tell you about fees or overages they receive beyond a straight percentage of rental income.
3. Have a preset spending limit without needing prior approval.
4. Have them provide statements that reveal expenses and income on a per-unit basis.
5. Receive and review monthly reports.

of Residential Property Managers (NARPM). Professional managers usually work for a percentage of the gross income, which is negotiable.

Banker. When you need money for major improvements or repairs, you may want to access money quickly. You may also need a bank document regarding your account or financial capability to be faxed on short notice. Developing relationships with top people at your local bank branch is always a good move. Get to know the branch manager on a first-name basis. Go in, introduce yourself, and touch base with this person *before* you actually need money or help. Let the banker know what you're doing so he or she can share your successes. When the time comes for needed funds or help in another way (e.g., a needed bank document faxed or a large check covered so it's paid and not returned), you'll already have a good relationship.

Mortgage lender. Good deals pop up all the time. When you want to put your hands on financing quickly to take advantage of a buying opportunity, having a relationship with a mortgage lender can make it possible for you to act fast, if necessary. A banker is limited in getting money to you only from the bank he or she works for, while a mortgage lender can independently get mortgage money from a variety of sources. Get prequalified so you know how much financing you can obtain as you make your purchasing plans.

Hard money lender. Money lenders lend money from their own funds or other private funds, and can offer quick financing to purchase and/or rehab properties. Obtaining funds from a hard money lender isn't contingent on personally qualifying for the loan as much as with a bank loan. Instead, it's based on using the property as collateral. But it costs more up front in "points" and higher interest rates than a bank or mortgage company. Consider this option only if you're using the money short term to buy, fix up, and then sell a property—or refinance more conventionally. You may find it allows you to get immediate control of a property and make a profit, even if financing costs are high. However, the profits are still high compared with not getting the property at all.

Business vendors and store managers. When owning rental property, you need supplies and materials from time to time. Keep records of the type of supplies you buy (e.g., paint, locks, appliances) and develop a relationship with store managers and vendors where you buy. Become a regular or "preferred" customer. Many vendors give preferred customers a minimum 10 percent discount. Always ask store managers and vendors you work with for a discount, especially as you become a loyal, valued customer.

Local landlords/investors. Joining a real estate association near you will be one of the smartest moves you'll make. Your nominal investment will quickly be surpassed by the benefits you receive. Other landlords and investors can be your best source for referrals, and you'll see them at meetings once a month. Identify a few who have like interests and goals, then meet with them outside the monthly meetings and offer each other encouragement. Along with support, your landlording buddies can offer practical assistance like referring overflow applicants to one another.

Other individuals worth knowing. Throughout my investing experience, receiving assistance from various individuals at critical times has saved me aggravation. It's worth the effort to develop positive working relationships with a local housing inspector and contacts at the courthouse, the Section 8 office, major utility companies, large employers in the area, and law enforcement agencies. These are just a few of the contacts that may prove helpful, if not essential, to you.

Buy a **R**olodex

One of the most practical and profitable tips I can offer is to buy and use a Rolodex or an electronic address book so you can keep *every* contact you make and need in your real estate and management endeavors. That resource will become one of your most valuable management tools over the years.

Board of advisors. Smart business owners recognize the value in seeking counsel from a board of seasoned advisors before making important decisions. Unfortunately, few real estate investors have set up a board of advisors for various reasons (e.g., it would cost too much to pay them, business owners aren't available, etc.). And for competitive reasons, successful colleagues in your field would be reluctant to share all of their best ideas. However, thanks to the power of the Internet, you can now tap into an awesome collective brain trust of some of the most successful landlords and managers in the country. They freely share counsel 24 hours a day, 7 days a week. Whenever you have an important management decision and want feedback from successful landlords and real estate investors, post a question at the MrLandlord.com Q & A Forum. In less than 1 hour, you'll get feedback and suggestions. Thousands check the Q & A Forum daily to ask and learn from this "board of advisors."

RESIDENTS

Your residents need to be seen as a vital part of your success team. Some landlords actually have a "me against them" mentality, which often means only one party can win. After years of owning properties and "battling" with residents, many landlords get burned out. That's no way to have fun and win in this business. Instead, implement a management approach so both parties can win! If residents feel that they can win in some ways, they'll be more likely to work *with* you, instead of *against* you, during the entire rental relationship. Ask for their feedback. Check with them periodically and systematically before making major rental decisions. For example, I seek their input on how much rent they want to spend, what property upgrades they'd like, and so on. If you do this, they feel like winners and you still enjoy your rental properties and real estate investing years from now. Chances are, you'll still be increasing your wealth, not just fighting to maintain it.

If you've owned properties for a few years and have already begun feeling burned out, I have good news. There's still hope for you, but you must change your ways of managing. This guide holds the keys to reviving your life as a real estate investor. It will help you gain greater cooperation from your current residents by meeting their needs while maximizing your profits.

Let's first discuss the last of the three preparatory steps for survival and success.

3

STUDY WHAT YOU MUST
KNOW TO SURVIVE

*"Whether you are experienced or inexperienced, you are dealing
with large sums of money in this business and you cannot
afford to be complacent or uninformed."*

—LEIGH ROBINSON

Real estate investing offers great rewards, financial and otherwise. However, you can't simply do whatever you wish to do when dealing with rental property or residents, even if it seems logical. For example, just because someone has not paid you rent for more than a month, you can't simply stop paying the utilities for that house. And though it's your house, you can't simply stop by whenever you wish and ask to look around just because you suspect something isn't right.

While this guide provides suggestions for the right steps to maximize income from your rental property, you don't want to take the wrong steps, which can cost you hundreds, thousands, or tens of thousands of dollars. In fact, certain wrong steps can cost you your property. Federal, state, and local laws and rules not only govern certain things you can (or can't) do, but what, how, and when certain actions and procedures must be taken.

Realize that many residents you deal with have been residents longer than you've been a landlord. A large percentage of them know how to "work" the system and rules to their advantage. They know their rights and what you're permitted to do. If you take a wrong step, residents may try to use that against you. That, too, can be costly. (Pay special attention to Step 5 regarding strategies to screen out potential problem residents.)

If you have been investing in real estate part-time for a while, use the information here as a checklist for studying topic areas and the "latest" rules, so you avoid making costly mistakes. For example, did you know that some landlords are getting sued because they use an answering machine or voice mail system to help screen their calls? They don't call back certain prospects, who in their opinion, sound like they wouldn't qualify. That's a common practice among landlords and seems logical. However, there's a name associated with that phone screening practice—linguistic profiling—which can be considered illegal discrimination, running afoul of fair housing laws.

The most important topics of study to stay updated on are highlighted here. Seek additional resources to stay updated in these areas. Even now, with more than 20 years' experience, I have to remind myself to stay up to date because the rules continually change. To help you know which areas to periodically pay attention to, here's a short list of "must-know" topics:

- Landlord-tenant state laws
- Security deposit guidelines
- Rules of eviction
- Lead-based paint disclosure
- Fair Housing Act
- Fair Credit Reporting Act
- Disability discrimination and service animals
- Section 8 rentals
- Local laws and requirements

LANDLORD-TENANT STATE LAWS

The landlord-tenant laws of your state cover all aspects of the rental business. Those laws ultimately govern the responsibilities and rights of both the landlord and the resident. That's why it's imperative to study these laws and make sure you're fulfilling your responsibilities as required by law. In this highly regulated business that's prone to lawsuits, you definitely don't want to find yourself at risk for not fulfilling your obligations.

These laws also explain what methods of remedy are available to you if your residents don't fulfill their obligations with the law and your agreement. You can probably get a complete copy of the landlord-tenant act and tenant laws for your state from either the state consumer protection agency or the attorney general's office. You can also find them at MrLandlord.com.

SECURITY DEPOSIT GUIDELINES

You have a right to collect a security deposit from residents to help you protect yourself against any possible losses. However, different states have different legal requirements and restrictions by which to abide. Many states limit the amount of security deposit you can collect. For example, the limit may be the equivalent of one month's rent. Some states require that you pay interest on the deposit and specify where or how the deposit is held. In addition, many states have a maximum time period for when the deposit must be returned to the resident after the rental relationship has been terminated, or provide an accounting for why the deposit isn't being returned. Noncompliance with these requirements can cost you the deposit and, in some states, double or triple the amount in damages—even if the resident left owing money or has damaged the property.

RULES OF EVICTION

Eviction laws vary from state to state, so learn the procedures and timetable for evictions in your area. Making one minor mistake in procedures or timing could cause your case to be dismissed, which is why studying this area is vital. To evict a resident, you must first serve a notice according to state law (e.g., a "Pay or Quit" notice). If the resident doesn't pay in full or move out within the specified time of the notice (also dictated by law), you commence eviction proceedings. You'd file a lawsuit, commonly called an "unlawful detainer" or "summary proceeding," which is a court order to remove the resident. Note: It's illegal to remove a resident or change the locks without going through a legal process, no matter how much money the resident has not paid.

The eviction process may take from 10 to 45 days, depending on your state and whether the resident creates delays by challenging your actions. Once a judge or court declares you the winner (called a judgment or order), a warrant (a *writ* in some states) is issued. This legal document directs a sheriff, marshal, constable, or other local official to remove the resident and possessions from the premises. In some areas, you're required to hire movers to remove possessions and then store the resident's property for a certain time before disposing of it. Check state statutes so you fully understand the eviction process.

Though not difficult to understand, landlord-tenant law is technical. A misstep in your paperwork or procedure could mean having your case thrown out and starting over. I regard using legal evictions as a last resort to dealing with nonpaying or nonconforming residents. (See Step 10 for an alternative approach.) The first time it becomes necessary to go through the legal eviction process, consider seeking the counsel of an attorney—a member of your success team—who specializes in landlord-tenant law.

FAIR HOUSING ACT

The Fair Housing Act prohibits discrimination in the sale, rental, lease, or negotiation for real property based on race, color, religion, sex, national origin, familial status, or handicap. It also prohibits discrimination in financing, blockbusting, and steering in relation to housing opportunities.

What is discrimination? A landlord may consider a number of criteria when selecting residents. Some criteria are legal, proper, and acceptable; other criteria are illegal, improper, and may not be an acceptable reason for denying someone housing. If an illegal or nonacceptable criterion is the basis for turning down an applicant, this is illegal discrimination. The landlord is guilty of an unfair or discriminatory practice. In this case, an applicant can file a discrimination charge and possibly win a lawsuit (some cases have resulted in multimillion-dollar judgments).

In addition to federal law, some states have added "protected" classes of individuals against whom you can't discriminate. To play it safe, I suggest you don't reject an applicant for any of these reasons: sex, race, religion, color, marital status, familial status, national origin, age, sexual orientation, source of income, or mental or physical disability. Additionally, don't turn people away because they're part of a designated group (e.g., specific occupation, welfare recipients, etc.). Decide on your criteria, write them down, and apply them to every prospective resident consistently. (See Step 5 for a sample set of criteria.)

Fair housing exceptions? Landlords who own one, two, or a few rental homes, or perhaps live in their small multifamily building, ask me if fair housing laws apply to them because they heard somewhere that some landlords are exempt. While limited exceptions exist, for the sake of your survival, I strongly suggest that you not look for possible exceptions. Why? Because increasingly the court system and judges are ruling in favor of residents and laws are conforming to enforcing fair housing policies on all landlords. Even if your state permits you, in your particular case, to discriminate against one of the protected classes, doing so is not worth the hassle, time, and money of having a discrimination claim filed against you. Instead, use the strategies in Steps 4 and 5 to attract, screen, and select qualified residents without need for exceptions or loopholes. You'll maintain your peace of mind and your cash flow will increase tremendously.

Note: Not only are you responsible for any discriminatory action you may take, but if others work with you to rent properties, you may be held liable for their actions as well. Give those who assist you—spouse, relative, friend, resident manager, handyman, neighbor, or resident—clear instructions on what to say and do when showing property to a prospective resident. No one should convey or imply to applicants that you illegally discriminate. (See Step 4 for instructions on what to say and do.)

FAIR CREDIT REPORTING ACT

The Fair Credit Reporting Act requires that landlords—if taking an "adverse action" (e.g., denying housing) against applicants based *in any way* on a consumer or credit report from a consumer reporting agency—provide an "adverse action notice" to that consumer. Specifically, the notice informs applicants about the adverse action, identifies the consumer reporting agency providing the report that contributed to the landlord's action, and specifies consumers' rights under the Fair Credit Reporting Act (FCRA).

Reports that landlords use to help them evaluate rental applications include:

- A credit report from a credit bureau, such as Trans Union, Experian, Equifax, or an affiliate company
- A report from a tenant-screening service, like one on MrLandlord .com that provides a credit report that the service obtained from a credit bureau; it also reports on an applicant's rental history

Common adverse actions by landlords include:

- Denying the application
- Requiring a cosigner on the lease
- Requiring a deposit that would not be required for another applicant
- Requiring a larger deposit than might be required for another applicant
- Raising the rent to a higher amount than for another applicant

A sample notice is included in the Appendix.

In fact, an adverse action notice is required even if information in the consumer report wasn't the main reason for the denial. If the information in the report plays a small part in the overall decision, the applicant must still be notified. Landlords who fail to provide these disclosure notices face legal consequences. The FCRA allows individuals to sue landlords for damages in federal court. A person who successfully sues is entitled to recover court costs and reasonable legal fees.

The law also allows individuals to seek punitive damages for deliberate violations of the FCRA. In addition, the Federal Trade Commission (FTC), other federal agencies, and the states may sue landlords for noncompliance and get civil penalties. If you have questions about the FCRA or would like to obtain a copy of the act, you can access it online at *http://www.ftc.gov.*

LEAD-BASED PAINT DISCLOSURE

Do you own and rent properties built before 1978? If so, a federal law requires that you give out a booklet called *Protect Your Family from Lead in Your Home* to anyone who rents your properties. You must have all adult residents sign a disclosure form as well. The Environmental Protection Agency (EPA) regulating this law provides these for free on its Web site *(http://www.epa.gov)* or you can obtain them at MrLandlord.com. All landlords of pre-1978 residential property must give the disclosure about lead-based-paint hazards to residents before signing the rental agreement. Those who fail to comply violate the Toxic Substances Control Act, which can result in a civil penalty of up to $11,000 for each violation.

In the rental agreement, the lessee must confirm receipt of a statement by the landlord disclosing the presence of known lead-based-paint hazards in the housing being leased or indicating no knowledge of the presence of lead-based paint and hazards. The landlord also must disclose information concerning known lead-based paint and/or lead-based-paint hazards, such as the basis for determining that lead-based paint and/or hazards exist, the location of the lead-based paint and/or lead-based-paint hazards, and the condition of the painted surfaces. Landlords must disclose a list of any records or reports available pertaining to lead-based paint and/or lead-based-paint hazards in the housing that have been provided to the lessee. If no such records or reports are available, the landlord shall indicate that.

If a rental agent is involved, include as an attachment or within the contract a statement that the agent has informed the landlord of his or her duties under the rule, and a statement by the agent that he or she is aware of the duty to ensure compliance with the rule. Include in the lease the signatures of the landlord, agent, and lessee certifying the accuracy of their statements, as well as dates. Retain a copy of the completed disclosure records for three years from the completion date of the lease or sale agreement.

Most states also have state lead hazard reduction laws and guidelines of which you need to be aware. The guidelines may include specific requirements and procedures regarding painting restrictions, inspection, testing, reporting, abatement, and licensing, or certification requirements for abatement contractors, plus owner responsibilities toward occupants in housing found to have hazardous findings, and so on.

DISABILITY DISCRIMINATION AND SERVICE ANIMALS

Although the subject of residents with disabilities is covered under the fair housing laws, studying this topic is worthwhile because many real estate investors may not think the same way the government does.

Federal law says a landlord is prohibited from discriminating against applicants who have a physical or mental disability that substantially limits one or more major life activities. The landlord cannot refuse to let residents make reasonable modifications to their dwelling or common use areas at the residents' expense. In addition, where reasonable, the landlord may permit changes only if the resident agrees to restore the property to its original condition. Further, landlords cannot refuse to make reasonable adjustments to the rules, procedures, or services in order to give them an equal opportunity to use a rental, including allowing special rent payment plans for residents whose finances are managed by a third party or government agency.

According to the Department of Housing of Urban Development (HUD), people with past drug addictions or recovering alcoholics are considered to have disabilities, therefore, you may not refuse to rent to someone on that basis—even if the addiction resulted in previous arrests and convictions.

Also, what some landlords call a pet, the government does not. You may or may not decide to permit residents to have pets in your properties. However, federal law dictates that you allow residents with disabilities to have service animals (e.g., seeing-eye dogs). Landlords may require documentation from an applicant's physician that an animal is needed and specifically trained to assist the resident. Legally, the service animal isn't considered a pet, so rules (e.g., additional deposit or monthly fees) for pet-owning residents may not apply.

SECTION 8 HOUSING

You may consider participating in the Section 8 program (Section 8 refers to Section 8 of the United States Housing Act of 1937). This HUD program is administered through local housing agencies. Residents with low income can qualify to participate in this program, which directly pays participating landlords a large percentage of rent on a Section 8 resident's behalf. Participating residents are responsible for paying a small percentage.

The advantage? Participating landlords can expect the government to pay rent directly and on time each month. Participating residents have a built-in incentive to pay their percentage or risk not only being removed from the property but from the Section 8 program altogether (though from the landlord's perspective, the removal process isn't always as easy as you'd expect).

The disadvantage? Being part of the program means your property is subject to additional governmental involvement and rules. For example, it has to pass an inspection annually and it's subject to government-set limits on the amount of rent you'd receive (which may or may not be equivalent to market rents in the area).

That said, thousands of landlords nationwide happily participate in the Section 8 program and I, too, have had success with it. Yet, I've also heard horror stories from participating landlords in different parts of the country about administrative problems and unreasonable inspection requirements. I suggest talking to participating landlords in your area to get their feedback because how the program is administered varies in different jurisdictions. Regarding problems with residents in the program, a lot falls back on the landlord's screening process. With good screening, your chances of finding a qualified applicant in the program are just as good as finding one outside it.

Note: While most states still give landlords the option of not participating in the Section 8 program, as of this writing a few states now dictate that landlords can't reject applicants solely because they're "Section 8" applicants. Stay abreast of rulings and procedures a landlord must follow regarding the Section 8 program in your area. To learn more, contact your local housing authority.

LOCAL LAWS AND REQUIREMENTS

"Do not pass GO. Do not collect $200." As you're on your way to "Monopoly" riches, you can't pass GO without learning about special "local" requirements for landlords in your area. For different reasons, more local jurisdictions are adding requirements beyond those that the federal or state laws may mandate. These requirements may include in-specting, permitting, and registration or licensing of rental properties with accompanying fees. Utility companies may also impose special re-quirements or fees for rental properties not imposed on owner-occupied dwellings in the same area.

Although there may be federal laws and state laws in place, don't as-sume there are no additional—even more stringent—local requirements dealing with the same issues. For example, in some areas, regulations re-garding lead-based paint are enforced more tightly at the local level. Even state landlord-tenant laws, eviction procedures, or discrimination issues may have local nuances or variances in the law that differ from the rest of the state. It also may be because certain laws or rulings are han-dled or interpreted differently by the courts in various jurisdictions.

Occupancy standards—the maximum number of residents allowed in a rental dwelling—can vary, and sometimes even within the same ju-risdiction. For example, if you rent properties near a college or univer-sity, you may face restrictions within a certain radius of the campus that only so many nonrelated adults can occupy a single dwelling. Local areas in a few states have rent control ordinances that limit the amount of rent to be charged. Note: Check this out if you have property in certain parts of California, District of Columbia, Maryland, New Jersey, or New York.

To help you stay updated on local rulings affecting landlords, join a local investor or landlord association. If there's no local association, find disgruntled landlords in the local courthouse doing evictions and start your own association. National Real Estate Investors Association can provide information and assist you in starting a local association.

OTHER AREAS WORTHY OF STUDY

To survive as a real estate investor with rental property, you need to keep learning. I suggest these additional topics are worth studying:

- Property acquisition and negotiation strategies (as you buy more rental property)
- Asset protection (if you have significant personal assets to protect from possible lawsuits)
- Employment and labor issues, including workers' compensation (if you hire a manager as an employee and not an independent

contractor). Note: Having residents work on your property is a gray area in which they could be legally seen as employees.

- Business marketing, salesmanship, profit building, and customer retention strategies

As a part-time real estate investor, learn how to run your properties in a businesslike manner by studying effective business principles in this guide and beyond it. I encourage you to note the business practices of other investors, of successful individuals, and of companies in various industries. Although the laws may change little in business practices, playing the game itself is always changing. In upcoming steps, you'll see many "new" ways to fill vacancies, maximize income, and retain residents that aren't like the "old" ways used by landlords who are growing frustrated because they're not getting the same quality residents and the same cash flow they used to. Yes, the rules are changing. And this guide gives you a new people-centered style of management to cope better in the 21st century.

Let me also help with transition issues that arise when a real estate investor takes over managing a rental property that has existing residents. This is followed by an essential checklist of the most costly management mistakes made by new and old real estate investors. Learn what to avoid and save yourself thousands of hours of frustration.

MANAGEMENT TRANSITION: TAKING OVER AS A NEW MANAGER

During the time that you invest in real estate, you'll buy properties that have no rental residents. As you do buy more, you'll fill the vacancies as quickly as possible with ideal residents and maximum rents. (See Step 4.)

Some properties you purchase, however, will have residents you inherit. While you may be the new owner of the property, also recognize that you are the manager as well. And using the manager title is how you should represent yourself to your residents.

I also suggest that, at a minimum, you create a "business" with a fictitious name to run your rental business. (At this point, I'm referring to a business with you as the sole proprietor.) I suggest, however, discussing with your attorney a different type of business structure to protect your assets. If your personal net worth is already substantial, don't wait to have this discussion—owning property in your own name leaves you at risk to lose your personal assets. Remember, you're a business, not a "mom and pop" landlord.

If You're New to Management . . .

With a businesslike approach in mind, set up a bank account in your business name and get a post office box. Request that all postal communication from residents be sent to your post office box address, and that rent checks be made payable to your business name and sent to your post office box. (See Step 7 for suggestions on preferred ways for accepting and collecting rent payments.)

I used to suggest that you get a second phone line for your rental business. Today, a better alternative communication is a dedicated cellular phone, now available for a low monthly cost. You'll find it helpful having a phone while traveling to and from properties, or responding to inquiries from wherever you are.

If you haven't yet, start using a property management software program and keep proper business records. Not keeping records can cost you a lot of time and money, especially at tax time. A software program can track records of your residents, along with all your rental-related income and expenses. That way, you can easily find and review these records when needed. Reviewing records periodically is a highly recommended management practice. It can tell you whether you're achieving your goals.

When You Inherit Residents . . .

If you're purchasing a property that already has residents, here are the seven action steps you should take:

1. Prepare a letter that introduces your management company, your role as manager, and your main win-win polices (which you'll read about in Step 6). When inheriting residents, any lease in effect with the former owners transfers to you. If residents were on

fixed-length year leases, you can't change major terms until their current lease expires. With month-to-month agreements, you still have to give the resident proper notice (in most states, 30 days) before changing any major terms of the agreement.

2. Before purchasing rental property with inherited residents, always ask for a copy of each resident's current rental agreement, original rental application, property condition checklist, and records regarding security deposit, payment history, or rental violations. Any information that the previous owner can provide could help you.

3. In your first communication with residents, come across in a businesslike manner. Communicate that you want to maintain a mutually beneficial, win-win relationship. Always see things from the residents' perspective. Don't make your communication one-sided. Mail this letter and mention in the letter that you will be stopping by to introduce yourself.

4. Within the first seven to ten days of taking over ownership of a property, plan a personal visit. If, for any reason, residents indicate that there are some things they need fixed or would like to see improved on the property, respond by saying this: "Our company will be glad to address your concerns. Because our company works on a priority basis, let me know at this time what would be the *one* most important thing that you'd like us to address now, so we can schedule for that concern to be addressed. Our company will also be doing periodic inspections of the property. We're looking to see that you're handling routine upkeep and maintenance. I'll make sure we take care of any property concerns that are the company's responsibility." This type of response not only deals with the customer's most pressing concern, but also establishes how maintenance matters will be handled.

5. Take care of major matters in a priority manner; don't handle every little concern, and take care of things in a systematic way based on your schedule. At the same time, expect the resident to handle routine upkeep and maintenance.

6. Let residents know the time frame in which you'll take care of their biggest concern (e.g., within the next two to four weeks), and also have them fill out a resident information sheet so you

have updated records on all residents (especially those who need work done on their property).

This information sheet need not be anything more than a rental application. Simply remove the word *application* from the top of the page and substitute the words *resident information*. Do you see how I'm setting the tone for how the relationship will work? That is, a resident requests something of you and you request something of the resident. Residents soon learn that if they're looking to you for something, that you only focus on important concerns, and that matters are handled based on your schedule (not the resident's whims), and that you also look to them for cooperation and assistance. Starting the relationship in this way helps significantly reduce (if not eliminate) frivolous or spontaneous requests during the rental term.

7. Do what's necessary to address the resident's most important concern within the promised time frame (the sooner the better). As implied earlier, don't try to deal with every matter residents may mention. Have them focus on their biggest concerns; never ask for a list of all the problems they may have. If you do, that sets up the relationship for disappointment because if you don't complete everything on the list, many residents remain unsatisfied. They will feel you are not doing your job. However, by having residents focus on one thing, it's easier to address that one concern and they'll see you as the hero. Starting off the relationship in this way makes it easier to take over as manager of a new house or building with residents you've inherited.

Raise the Rent Now or Later?

The question often comes up about raising rents as soon as legally permissible with inherited residents—especially if rent amounts are below market rates. I suggest that if they need to be raised (and the residents are on a month-to-month agreement), ask the "seller" of the property to send out a rent increase letter *before* you close on the property and take over ownership. The rent increase letter states that the new rental amount will take place in the next 60 days. In this way, let the seller be seen as the bad guy, not you. Instead, you come in as the hero ready to promptly take care of the one big concern each resident has.

A lot of your success in managing people is not doing a lot of work but simply knowing what actions to do, and do them in the most effective way possible. Success also means not doing the wrong things, which brings me to a list I'd like to share before going in depth into the action steps and strategies. As you deal with different aspects of the rental business, it's good to know which mistakes have been made by other investors so you can avoid them. Study and review this list twice a year.

TEN MOST COMMON AND COSTLY MANAGEMENT MISTAKES

Mistake 1: Not Reviewing State Landlord-Tenant Laws

Landlords generally don't read and familiarize themselves with the landlord-tenant laws of their state. You've already been warned and advised earlier: Study the landlord-tenant laws for your state. You can't know all your rights or responsibilities and proper procedures without first learning the laws. Remember, the courts don't consider ignorance a valid excuse. Unfortunately, too many landlords never review the laws and their negligence comes back to haunt them. Get a copy of your state's landlord-tenant laws and get to know them.

Mistake 2: Not Running Their Rentals Like a Business

Landlords tend to run things more on the "handshake principle" and assume people will do the right thing. That sounds good in theory, but that's not how you run a business in today's world. If you were to go into any major store and buy something on credit, the storeowner or manager doesn't simply shake your hand. Someone takes the time to clearly communicate the agreement you are entering into and your responsibilities, and any needed agreements, addendums, and disclosures are agreed to and signed and copies given. Nothing is assumed.

In the rental business, in essence, you're extending a large amount of credit to your customers (several thousands of dollars to be paid over the year in rent payments). Therefore, you should be taking time to clearly communicate and address issues with new residents. Various agreements, addendums, and disclosures are needed to run your rental operation in an efficient, professional manner. This is a business, and only the landlord who treats it that way will be successful.

Need more guidance? Pick up a copy of my previous book titled *The Landlord's Kit,* which includes over 150 rental forms to help you run your business and communicate to your residents in almost every possible rental situation.

Mistake 3: Poor Recordkeeping

Sloppy records lead to lost tax advantages and lost profits from not properly monitoring activities and results. Poor recordkeeping can lead to trouble with residents and the law if you did not follow through on actions because they weren't properly noted or acted on in a timely manner. Obtain a management software program to help you maintain your records.

Mistake 4: Not Asking Enough for Rent

This refers to owners who shortchange themselves in two ways. One way is the typical landlord who remains silent and doesn't raise the rent annually because the resident is a "good" resident and doesn't bother the landlord with problems. The trouble with this "silent" form of management is that the good residents often don't bother landlords for repairs or maintenance because they don't want to ruffle feathers and have rents raised. This is a formula for disaster. The secret to keeping good residents is *not* by keeping rents low. (See Step 9 for secrets on keeping good residents, including how to raise the rents so you don't lose them. In fact, you'll learn how to get residents to become happier each year they stay with you.)

Landlords also shortchange themselves by not implementing policies that can boost the amount of "base rent" new residents and continuing residents are willing to pay, not even referring to annual rent increases. (Highlight many points when you read Step 8 discussing almost 100 ways to maximize your rental income.)

Mistake 5: Not Being Proactive in Performing Preventive Communication

Many landlords wait until something breaks or until residents say they're moving before they pay attention. It's a time-consuming, frustrating, and costly way to run a rental business, yet that's how most landlords operate. That's not how you will operate now that you have this guide. From the next step until the end of this book, you'll learn to use preventive communication to get residents to not only stay with you but also become customers for life.

Mistake 6: Hiring the Wrong People or Not Enough People

Trying to save money by hiring someone who charges less for their professional services or performs discounted repairs, maintenance, and improvements can be the most expensive option in the long run. However, landlords who do everything themselves only limit their profit and growth. Identify and use a network of professionals, contractors, and vendors (suggested in Step 2) and you'll be glad you did.

Mistake 7: Not Improving The Property

Improvements such as painting the exterior or offering a choice of wall color in one of the rooms, installing new carpet or ceramic tile, or adding fixtures and upgrades in a rental unit almost always brings excellent dividends to the owner (especially in response to requests by residents willing to pay more for such improvements). Too many landlords, however, don't take the initiative soon enough and continually lose some of their best customers.

Mistake 8: Renting to Family Members or Friends

It is normally recommended *not* to rent to family members or friends because many, if not most, individuals can't separate a business relationship from a personal one. Thus, when rules aren't followed and "business" actions must be taken, people tend to want the other party not to adhere to strict business policies, but be lenient because of the personal relationship. And when there's no leniency, individuals get upset and the personal (family or friendship) relationship is damaged. Often that relationship is never the same. Then, not only does the business relationship end, but the personal relationship often ends, too. Only relatively few individuals can keep business as business and always follow your rules. Under normal circumstances, sooner or later, a rule gets broken and an issue must be dealt with. Unless you want to take the high risk of damaging a personal relationship, don't rent to friends or family members.

Mistake 9: Not Exchanging Information with Other Landlords to Continue to Educate Yourself

Why do people continue to reinvent the wheel when others have already learned so much? Facilitating an exchange of information is one of the main reasons landlord associations exist. Get to know other landlords. Attend real estate conferences and exchange experiences and ideas. In addition, the *biggest* exchange of information among rental owners takes place every day on the largest landlord forum on the Internet. Every day, thousands of owners exchange valuable tips, management secrets, and solutions to fellow landlords on the MrLandlord.com Q & A Forum.

Congratulations. You've taken a BIG step in your education process by purchasing or borrowing this guide. (Note: If this is a borrowed copy, I'm sure you realize you actually need your own so you can make notes in the margins. This is a manual you'll use over and over again.)

Also attend seminars, read newsletters, and keep abreast of each of the areas noted here. Without question, the most successful real estate investors are those who continually educate themselves. And the ones who complain about problems have stopped learning the latest strategies for success.

Mistake 10: Not Fully Screening Applicants

Of all the mistakes made, according to several surveys done through MrLandlord.com, not fully screening applicants is the number one most common mistake made by landlords. There are numerous reasons why, from simple laziness to the typical statement, "The person seemed okay." It's not that no screening was done; it's that the landlords didn't do *all* their normal screening procedures. Perhaps they felt the credit check wasn't necessary, or they didn't call the references to verify all the information on the application.

Can you guess how most landlords realize they made this mistake? Yes, after they accept the resident and the resident turns out to be bad. That's a costly way to learn from a mistake, but almost all landlords have learned this lesson the hard way. Occasionally, you can get away with not fully screening and the resident turns out okay. But, the one time it doesn't work out can cost you dearly—thousands of dollars plus horror stories of nonpayment and property damage. A poorly selected resident can cause "good" neighboring residents to move and force you to go through an eviction process. It's not worth the risk.

Always perform a complete screening procedure on applicants. While this may sound difficult, I have good news. There is a simple yet effective screening procedure suggested and included in Step 5, along with numerous screening tips and questions so that you will be able to screen out potential problem residents and avoid over 90 percent of the problems other landlords face.

This survival guide won't let you down. It will become your best friend. Refer to it continually, especially whenever you need tips to fill a vacancy and definitely when you are selecting and screening rental applicants.

SEVEN ACTION STEPS

4

FILL A VACANCY WITH THE IDEAL RESIDENT

"I've learned that just getting a property rented is not the right objective. I now look for the right occupant for the rental. If you wait for a good fit, it seems to last longer."

—DAVID DOYLE

Let me put forth this challenge to you. If you follow the recommended action steps outlined in Step 4, I guarantee you'll rent any vacancy you have within the next 30 days.

Your ultimate goal isn't just to fill your vacancy fast, but to fill it fast with an ideal or qualified resident. In this step, you'll discover innovative, practical, and proven ideas to help you rent your properties faster. I encourage you to highlight the strategies you think will be most effective for you and your rental market. Make notations right in this guide and mark or underline suggestions you want to implement. Let this guide serve as a checklist to use whenever you need to fill a vacancy. In the process, you're building a game plan of effective strategies that you can implement yourself or give to an assistant or manager. You don't want your properties sitting empty.

Why do some landlords take so long to fill a vacancy? One reason is because they present their properties as an "average" home or apartment available for any average resident. That's not how smart businesses design and promote their products. They consider the customers they want to reach, design their product with those customers in mind, and then promote to those customers.

When competition is high and people have lots of rentals to choose from, consider whether yours is seen by prospects as an average home with no special appeal. If it is, there's no big incentive for them to rent from you versus from a landlord down the street.

Today's consumers (at least the "ideal" residents who pay top-market rents and stay long term) look for better-than-average homes. This holds true for all economic levels—low, middle, and high—in all types of neighborhoods. Quite simply, if your property is average in a competitive market, it will be hard to attract anything but average residents who only stay about a year, bringing with them typical resident problems.

People fill out rental applications because they perceive they're getting something other than what they can find elsewhere or they see something in the home that they like. I want to increase the odds that they'll see something in my rentals they like, that they'll perceive the home isn't just average. When preparing my property for showing, I do *not* start fixing it up based on what *I* think is appealing. I conduct surveys with customers to find out what features *they* like in their homes or would want added as part of a "custom rental home" package. Then I make sure those features or upgrades are offered in properties I'm preparing for rent. These features may include certain types of kitchen countertops, grab bars in the bathroom, washers and dryers, motion sensor lights outside the door, water filter systems, ceiling fans, choice of garden plants, Internet service, and so on.

Identifying the exact features that "my" residents and prospective residents may like is great for me. However, the question you must answer is: What features do your prospective residents like? Please don't miss the awesome marketing concept I'm sharing. The steps I suggest to market a product (in your case, a home or apartment) echo what successful businesses in all industries do.

I. Determine What Target Markets You'd Like to Reach

For example, I target people who work. (Later, I point out several target markets that are favorites of other landlords.)

Please note: Target marketing does *not* mean you're excluding, giving preference to, or denying anyone or any group the right to apply. Target marketing simply means you advertise in different places where chances are high you'll reach those who either will like the properties you have available (because of features offered or perhaps location) and/ or who are financially stable, property-responsible, or long-term residents. However, you should always allow anyone who expresses interest to apply for your property so you won't get into trouble from a fair housing standpoint. In any advertisement that you place, always promote the "features" of the property. Never include anything in your advertisements regarding "whom" the property is for because that would leave the impression you give preferential treatment. Take this a step further: I recommend you include the following line in your flyers, promotions, and Web site advertisements: *We are an equal opportunity housing provider, and we rent our homes without regard to race, color, religion, national origin, marital or familial status, sex, or physical disability.*

2. Find Out What Appeals to Your Prospective Customers

Not only can you ask current residents what appeals to them, but also ask prospective residents by putting this question right on your rental application: What is one feature or amenity you like best at your current home? Learn from the strategies of other successful real estate investors. That way, you can offer "custom home packages," which include one or two property features or incentives that appeal to residents in your area.

3. Take Your Advertising Directly to Where Your Target Markets Will See It: Where They Work, Shop, or Socialize

When prospective residents see your advertising and come to your rentals, you want them to see something in your homes that they like— or at least a list of options they'd like—to increase the likelihood they'll fill out an application. Most landlords are happy if 20 percent of prospective residents fill out an application. I want over 50 percent. Don't take offense, but if you limit how you prepare your properties to just what you think is appealing, you greatly reduce the number of prospects who will want it—and reduce your cash flow potential.

Instead of upgrades and features, you can also offer other move-in incentives that appeal to your target market. Many working people (again, one of my target markets) are concerned with the price of gasoline needed to get to work. Instead of offering a reduced rental rate as a move-in incentive, why not offer free gas?

Here's how this marketing idea can work. Meet with the owner or manager of the local gas station close to your rental and buy gas cards/certificates in $25 increments. In all your rental advertisements, include this phrase: Free Gasoline for Renters! Also ask permission to post a flyer about your free gasoline offer at each of the gasoline pumps. You can promise to purchase a dozen or more gas certificates (for example, 12 per rental). Every person who stops to buy gas at that location will see your flyers and wonder about getting free gas. Your promotion promises to give gas cards to new residents as a move-in gift and as a bonus to those who pay rent on time. Once residents move in, for each month they pay their rent on time, they get a free gas card. With this strategy, more "working people" will see the Free Gas flyers at the nearby gas station than a lot of other advertising you can do. This strategy gets prospects to think of you because no other landlord offers free gas.

Another landlord used the same idea by working with a shoe store owner after discovering her customers and target market liked shopping

No Money in the Budget

A property manager asked me, "What if there's no money in the budget for adding or offering something extra, and all that I have to work with is a 'standard' home or apartment? How can I advertise my standard apartments?"

It's amazing how some don't realize that money *will* be spent or lost one way or another. First of all, money is probably being spent for advertising of some kind because people see that as a "normal" expense. For most landlords, it's money wasted. They put their advertising dollars into newspaper ads that draw people to the rental, only to have their prospects feel reluctant to apply. Spend part of that advertising money on doing something "extra" so when prospects come by, they actually *want* to rent from you. Remember, each vacancy costs landlords between $800 and $1,500 dollars in turnover costs. Spend a little on something *extra* to rent the place faster, instead of sitting there losing money with an empty "standard" home. Make sure that your something "extra" really appeals to your target market.

at a particular upscale store nearby. The landlord offered "free shoes" as a move-in gift.

Whether you offer free gas, free shoes, a water filter system, or a maintenance guarantee, I want to stress this marketing point: Your goal is to make your properties and marketing different than what's found in the standard rental, so you can stand out among your competition.

4. Get the Word Out about Your Homes—and What's Special about Them—to Key Community Contacts

Use a network of community contacts to help you reach your target markets. The goal is not for *you* to put out a lot of marketing pieces over town. If that's all you do, you'll run yourself ragged. You're a part-time real estate investor; I don't want to give you extra work. Instead, develop key relationships with influential individuals who come in contact with the same markets that you're targeting. With many individuals helping you, it takes a lot less work on your part. For example, if you want to

Keep the Phone Ringing

As your "network" builds, use it as your primary source of lead generation instead of newspaper ads (which can be costly without generating results). When needed, For Rent signs and ads can be the supplemental or secondary source for generating calls. One real estate investor uses a wide network of business associates to keep her properties filled. All her former banker friends know she rents houses and they refer clients to her. Now in the field of medicine, she can contact the staff member who edits the hospital employee bulletin and place an ad directed at nurses, doctors, and staff. She can also post signs at the hospital, in the university faculty lounges, and on bulletin boards. She tells professors who always know post-graduates or fellows looking for a nice place. Her real estate agent friend helps with referrals and tells other agents. Her husband posts vacancies on the boards at the factories he visits through his business. Many friends take flyers home so their spouses can post flyers where they work also. This is an excellent example of developing a "marketing network" that keeps the phone continually ringing.

reach teachers or parents, a key contact could be the principal of a local school. Give a donation to the school when you rent to someone who heard about it through the school (e.g., from a letter sent to the faculty and parents).

Follow the suggested action steps and let them serve as a checklist of effective strategies that you can easily implement whenever you have a vacancy. Complete these steps and you will fill your vacancies.

I. KNOW YOUR MARKET—DO YOUR HOMEWORK

I suggest putting these ideas into motion to understand the market you serve.

1. Know What Your Residents Like

Conduct a survey and ask your current residents what features they like best about your property. Ask current residents what features of your rental made them originally decide to rent. Then make property additions or adjustments (if appropriate and within cash-flow reason) to make your property appealing to future prospects.

2. Know What Competing Houses and Apartments Have to Offer

To determine what other choices your prospective residents have, call and visit other rental homes and apartments advertising vacancies near your rental. Understand the advantages and disadvantages of each property you visit. Prepare a positive response that you will use to counter any objections a prospect may have when comparing your rental with others.

I suggest taking a day or evening to pose as a prospective resident. By doing this, you'll learn a tremendous amount about effective and noneffective ways to market in your area. This kind of training should benefit any landlord looking for ways to fill vacancies.

3. Review Ads in the Local Sunday Paper

Look at the Sunday real estate section of your local paper and see how others are marketing their rental properties through their classified ads. Have you overlooked using eye-catching phrases in your ad that you're reading in others? Next, cut out classified ads that look good and that describe rentals similar to yours. Then put these ads in a scrapbook and use the best ones as references when writing your own.

4. Survey Residents of Apartments to Learn Their "Satisfaction" Level

Send direct mail "satisfaction" surveys to residents of apartment buildings in the same general area of your rental properties. It's important that this type of correspondence look professional and not like the work of some desperate landlord just trying to steal residents. These surveys are especially useful when your competitors' properties are newer, fancier, or somehow appear better than your own rentals.

On the survey form you send, ask simple questions such as: What do you like most about your present apartment? What do you dislike most about your apartment? What would you change about your apartment or how it's managed? You may find their answers astounding and revealing. Their responses give you the exact type of information needed to position your rentals better and compete against nearby options. What's more, the complaints on these satisfaction surveys tell you exactly what your competitors' weaknesses are.

II. PREPARE YOUR PROPERTY

It's important to have your rental units 100 percent ready—100 percent repaired and 100 percent cleaned—for move-in when showing them to prospective residents. These factors actually persuade prospects more than price.

The following issues are also important.

1. Use Fresh Paint

Pay attention to the cosmetic factors such as fresh paint on the walls. Especially repaint all interior walls that are marginal. Cut the grass and have attractive landscaping.

Make the exterior of the rental building look as inviting as its interior. At a minimum, paint the exterior front porch and wash down the front side of the building, if needed. Wash the front windows so they sparkle.

2. Make Sure the Carpet and Flooring are In Good Condition

Clean existing carpets or even consider dying them. Certainly replace any worn-out carpets. You might even put down new ceramic flooring where needed.

3. Add Touches of Elegance

Think about providing little extras to make it more inviting, even if it's in a low-income neighborhood. For example, you could put up an attractive ceiling fan to add elegance to a main room.

People do notice details. Inexpensive brass switch plate covers give a room a finished look. So does putting brass kick plates on the front door. Add new doorknobs to make a front door look cleaner and bedroom doors look better. Replace old kitchen floors with ceramic tile for about the same price as vinyl. Use inexpensive miniblinds to cover windows. Dress up the exterior of the building with a fancy doorknocker, decorative porch light, simulated brass house numbers, and window shutters.

4. Light Up the Place

A greatly overlooked selling point is lighting. Wash your windows, keep the shades up during showings, and make sure there's a bulb in every light fixture. Use 60- or 100-watt bulbs if your fixtures will handle them. A brightly lit house or apartment looks welcoming.

5. Cleanliness Is Critical

Never show a dirty home. Before beginning to show your rental property to prospects, hire a professional team to clean the place thoroughly, including the windows, bathrooms, kitchen, appliances, light fixtures, floor, and so on. Make sure everything sparkles.

Because of the growing competition of home cleaning franchises, prices have become cost-effective and their professional teams can clean homes in just a few hours. It's worthwhile to hire them; it means you can begin showing your property sooner, rent it faster, and start receiving cash quicker. Not only that, a sparkling clean home attracts a better class of residents who appreciate cleanliness and who'll be more inclined to maintain the property.

Overall cleanliness of the property is important, but pay special attention to making sure the bathrooms and kitchen are super clean. The way your appliances look is especially important. Clean, new-looking appliances make a kitchen look inviting.

Two absolute essentials:

1. Pick up trash, rubbish, or any eyesores from around the property.
2. Remove all personal belongings of the previous resident if the property is vacant. (Be sure to discard it in the proper legal manner.)

6. Use the Right Smells to Increase Appeal to Prospects

Not only should the place be clean, but it should *smell* clean and even enticing. I have been in model homes that smell like apple pie, cinnamon rolls, freshly brewed coffee, and microwave popcorn.

Studies show that using scents in the rooms can increase the likelihood that prospective residents will want to rent the property. Make sure the scent you select appeals to prospective customers. Test different scents with prospective and current residents, all the while tracking the comments they make.

Before showing a property, make sure you clear the air, open the windows, and give the place a pleasant smell. Try these ideas:

• Light a scented candle. (Many scent options are available.)

- Paint one wall or even a closet door to create the smell of fresh paint.
- Use a cleanser with lemon or pine scent.

7. Exterminate Bugs before Showing Your Units

Even if you don't see bugs or rodents in your units, spend a few dollars to "bomb" your rentals for pests before you show them. Any landlord who has witnessed a prospective resident seeing a roach run out of the refrigerator during a showing knows how important this extermination step is. Don't risk that embarrassment.

III. REDUCE TURNOVER TIME

Here are a few strategies to avoid experiencing gaps between when current residents move out and new ones move in.

1. Offer an Incentive to Get Cooperation from Departing Residents

When it's time for residents to relocate at the end of their rental term, I ask them if I may start to show the house they're vacating a few weeks before they move out. I even offer a $50 bonus on top of their security deposit return if I rent the property before the resident's last day of occupancy. In case a prospective resident stops by unexpectedly, they'll usually even show it for me to help me rent it immediately. There's a $50 incentive to do so!

2. During the Advertising Phase, Always Stay Accessible

Can prospects reach you throughout the entire day or evening to ask about renting your home? If it's not easy to reach you, they won't waste their time with you and they'll contact other landlords. Plan ahead and, if necessary, hire a person to answer your phone during the days your ad runs in the newspaper. Give the person you hire a script to follow to prevent facts and intentions from being misunderstood.

Not only do you (or someone you trust) need to be accessible during the day but it's also important to be available to answer the phone and show rentals to prospects who can only visit during the evenings (until 8:00 PM) or early in the morning.

If the ads instruct people to call your phone number and you're on the go, at a minimum, put your cell number in your ads so you can be reached. Some landlords even put their digital pager number in their ads so that they can promptly return calls from interested prospects.

3. Provide Lead Time in Your Advertising

Start preparing for attracting new residents by advertising as soon as you get confirmation of your upcoming vacancy. Most responsible residents don't wait until they "have to have a place" before looking for a new rental. They start looking at least four to eight weeks in advance. You want to attract responsible residents, so the more lead time you can provide in your advertising, the better.

4. Set Up Lease Dates to Expire On the 25th of the Month, Not the Last Day of the Month

Some landlords set up their rental dates to run from the 25th to the 24th of each month. That way, when residents do move, they move out by the 24th of the month instead of the very end. Generally, that means your property would get advertised on the market ahead of everyone else's and is therefore available to rent sooner. By doing this, you lessen the competition you'll have when renting and you'll also collect rent sooner. That's good for your cash flow!

IV. REACHING TARGET MARKETS

To target your ideal customers, you need to identify them. This list includes just a few examples of different customers who've worked out well, for both me and other rental owners, and the accompanying strategies to attract these customers.

Employees working nearby. Contact employers within two miles of where you own rental property. Ask if you can put a flyer on a bulletin board, or if a letter can be given or sent to all employees regarding the properties you have available. Offer a donation to employers ($50 or $100) for charities of their choice if their employees rent any of your units. I think you'll find this approach is less expensive than running ads in the newspaper, which is often money wasted. If a large business has an employee newsletter, inquire about advertising in it and offer a discount for your rental in your advertisement.

Government workers. For example, if you want to attract workers at a large postal facility, mention the proximity of the facility to your properties in your flyers and ads.

Medical workers. Advertise in hospital employee bulletins and on boards around the building.

Empty nesters. Many people in the baby boom generation who have raised their children in homes and want to live their lives with fewer home-care responsibilities turn to apartment rentals. In fact, this "empty nester" group is one of the fastest-growing segments of renters in the United States. They have old-fashioned values and enjoy the opportunity to feel active and useful. For example, in some communities, empty nesters can be found at neighborhood bingo halls on a particular night of the week. Offer a donation to the organization sponsoring the bingo games and $50 worth of free bingo games as a move-in gift to qualified applicants.

Because mobility can be a problem, offer grab bars in the bathrooms as an optional feature. Or provide plenty of lighting and locks to make residents feel safe. You could even offer to install additional lighting as a move-in gift.

Working professionals. Be prepared to respond promptly to the maintenance requests of working professionals, or at least offer a maintenance guarantee. They expect you to stay on top of your business. (Precisely for this reason, some landlords avoid this group.) One way to attract this group is to make deals with local fitness clubs, which also target working professionals. Work out an advertising trade; the clubs allow you to post a flyer on their bulletin boards and you promote their gyms by giving flyers to all residents and prospective residents.

Handyman type. Attract this type of renter by advertising at local hardware stores. Also, go to a general contractor's work site during the workers' lunch break and pass out rental information, flyers, or cards to them.

Military personnel. List your rental with military housing offices in your area. It's not difficult with these customers to set up automatic payroll deduction to pay rent. And whenever there's a problem, the commanding officer might assist to remedy the matter.

Law enforcement personnel. To help prevent or reduce illegal activities from taking place in your buildings, contact all law enforcement agencies in your area (e.g., police department, sheriff office, FBI, etc.) and let them know you have properties available to rent.

Section 8 qualifiers. Contact the local housing authority and ask to be included on the list of landlords who accept Section 8 residents.

Teachers or parents at nearby schools. Ask if you can sponsor a PTA meeting or run an ad in the schools' football or athletic programs. Doing this is relatively inexpensive and readers are already familiar with the area.

Residents with special needs. One landlord I know owns properties near the airport. Residents constantly moved out of it because of unrelenting airplane noise. Realizing a couple of residents had been there a long time, she found out they stayed because they were hearing impaired; the noise didn't bother them. She decided to seek out more hearing-impaired individuals. She found out where they held meetings, attended a few, and then took the opportunity to invite attendees to consider living in her building.

She also learned what publications hearing-impaired individuals read and advertised in them. At her property, she changed doorbells from chimes to flashing lights to make the complex more attractive to this group. Today, she has a waiting list of hearing-impaired individuals who want to live in her rental homes. Another option for landlords with rentals near an airport is to target their marketing toward locally based flight attendants or airport employees.

There are many groups who may have special needs of one kind or another and other than physical. Some landlords reach out to different groups who may be overlooked by other rental owners. Those same landlords discover that various community and government agencies are actually looking for housing providers to direct individuals to and will even be responsible for the rent payments of the residents. For example, one landlord I know rents to individuals who are recovering from drug addiction. A former addict himself, he works with a local agency, he has plenty of applicants to select from, his properties stay filled, and the rent is automatically paid at a higher than market rate. Sure, there are other challenges that need to be addressed at times, and this is not a suggestion for every landlord to pursue.

The bigger point is that because of your background, past experiences, or unique training, you may feel at ease renting to individuals to whom other landlords are not reaching out. Another quick example is a landlord who is a war veteran and reaches out to veterans. Plus, you can have the rent payments come directly from a government agency.

I'm sure you get the idea. You may find that it's worth considering serving a market niche ignored by others that will not only keep your properties filled, but provide a needed service.

College students. Landlords who own property near a university often contact different segments of the student population and determine the procedure for promoting the housing they have available. For example, some landlords reach out to international students, others to graduate students or nursing students. If zoning laws or occupancy limits permit, renting a single family home to three to eight students can generate double or maybe even triple the amount of rent that can normally be received. Free Internet access appeals to many in this market.

Corporate leasing and/or high-income residents. Consider promoting "executive suites" directly to any nearby large corporations. What some landlords do is actually contract with the corporation, which then has staff members contact the owner or manager when an employee needs to move in on a short-term or long-term basis. To make the property appealing to corporate or high-income individuals, consider including in the rental rate some of the following options or services: weekly housecleaning, high-speed Internet access, answering service, lawn care, garage door openers, and the option to pay rent by credit card. For services offered, coordinate these with third-party providers.

V. TEST MARKETING AND ADVERTISING STRATEGIES

Put these strategies into motion to test your marketing.

1. Get to Know Businesses Located Within a Few Blocks of Your Property

People enjoy looking at flyers on bulletin boards at their places of work or in cafeterias. Ask to place index cards (use bright colors, not white) or flyers containing rental home information at companies near your rental property. Also request whether a letter that you draft promoting your nearby properties can be given or sent to each employee. Even ask if you can have five minutes at an upcoming employee meeting where you can communicate directly with the employees. Offer to donate $50 or $100 to those companies or their favorite charities in exchange for this access.

2. Hand Out Lots of Business Cards

Print business cards advertising that you rent apartments or homes, and then give them out generously to individuals you meet. Talk with large numbers of people in their regular course of business, including mail carriers, motel clerks, gym and spa managers, sales reps, and real estate agents.

3. Give Rental Information in Your Voicemail Message

On your voicemail message, remind callers that you have properties available for rent, and then provide a few details.

4. Organize a Garage Sale

Have a garage sale at your property and post a large sign that reads: ASK ABOUT THE APARTMENT OR HOUSE—IT'S AVAILABLE, TOO! Lots of people will be curious to look through the property. Even if they aren't interested in moving, give them a flyer. When your rental looks good, they're likely to call a friend or relative who may be interested.

5. Be a Guest Presenter

Find college classes, adult education courses, or community or civic groups that welcome guest speakers and offer a presentation on the subjects of making the most out of renting, how to find the best places to rent, or choosing the best type of rental home or apartment. After speaking, leave a piece of your literature with the students or those in attendance so they can contact you about renting opportunities. Also speak on local talk-radio programs, answering questions about what to look for and how to select your next rental home.

6. Get to Know Publications in Your Area and Advertise

Find apartment-hunter guides distributed free to prospective residents and list your property. Find out about small newspapers or rental guides in your area that offer free or low-cost advertising, and then run an ad continually.

7. Test a "Higher" Price

If your rental looks clean and you're attracting prospects but none are taking it, raise your price before dropping it. You see, entirely different sets of prospects look at properties at different price points. With your current price, those who are attracted to that level of pricing may not appreciate what you've done to the property (because they are only concerned about price, not value). At a higher price, you may be surprised that those looking at apartments or houses in that price range better appreciate it and willingly pay for what you offer. If that doesn't work, you can always go back and drop your price.

VI. MARKETING HELP FROM OTHERS

Turning to others to help fill vacancies has worked well for me over the past two decades. Here are several ideas I've used.

1. Get Help from Current Residents

Encourage good residents to spread the word about your vacancies by offering them a bonus (e.g., a free property upgrade or referral reward) for recommending a coworker, friend, or relative to sign a lease. To entice any referred prospects, offer the referred residents a discount on the first month's rent.

2. Get Help from Prospective Residents

Don't miss opportunities for referrals even from prospective residents. On your rental application, ask for the following information: The name and phone number of at least one friend, coworker, or colleague who also may be looking for a place to rent.

Create a Resident Referral Rewards Program

Offering a free upgrade referral program for finding qualified prospects has been highly successful for me. With this program, my current residents can get a free upgrade of their choice if they recommend a resident who meets my minimum criteria.

It's important that you remind residents at least quarterly of any referral reward program you offer. For example, I'm a frequent flyer on Delta Airlines, but Delta does not trust that I'll remember its frequent flyer program. It reminds me systematically. As a result, when I need to decide what airline to fly, chances are I'll go with Delta. Similarly, when you implement a strategy, your residents need to be reminded systematically of your free referral rewards program.

Always send a thank-you note to anyone who sends a referral, even if the person referred doesn't rent from you. You want residents to feel good about taking time to make referrals.

3. Get Help from Neighbors

Have flyers distributed on the same street as your rental or nearby streets, advertising the home or unit you have available. Your flyer can even include a P.S. that you also *buy* properties, and you'd be glad to discuss offers if owners might be selling their homes in the near future. Doing this invites the possibility that people with houses or multifamily buildings might contact you.

4. Find "Buddy" Landlords to Learn From and Share Information

I suggest developing a relationship with one or two successful landlords in your area who seem to keep their rentals filled. Ask if you can be present during a time when they are showing the rental property to a prospect. Take note of how they handle the showing process. Even ask if they would watch as you show your place to prospects and offer a friendly critique. In addition, ask your landlord buddies to refer any "overflow" of rental applicants to you.

5. Get Help from Local Businesses

Ask local merchants if you can post a rental flyer in their waiting areas. Include businesses such as barbershops, salons, specialty shops, dental or medical offices, restaurants, etc. Some merchants may also be willing to let you leave flyers on their store counter or tables. Purchase "Take One" display boxes to set on their counters and put your flyers in there.

Make an agreement to buy $25 or $50 gift certificates from any local merchant who refers a new resident to you. Then use the certificate as an incentive to prospective residents. Also ask merchants if you can include a flyer or letter with their monthly invoices to customers.

6. Get Help from Nearby Corporations

Directly contact personnel or training directors of large companies about the possibility of providing short-term or long-term, company-paid rentals for their personnel. Or let them know you have rental properties available for new employees moving into the area. Offer a special moving allowance to the company.

7. Get Help from Community Groups

Make a list of community groups, civic leagues, and service clubs in your area and get to know their leaders. Attend their meetings and talk about your rental properties. Pass out flyers and ask to make an announcement. You may even find it worthwhile to join one or more of these groups.

8. Get Help from Real Estate Agents

One landlord admits that whenever he has a vacancy, the first people he alerts are the real estate agents he works with in the area. They often know people who have difficulty qualifying to buy a property but may need housing right away. Agents could also put you in touch with prequalified prospective residents who may be ideal prospects for purchasing your property, if that's what you ultimately want. Although most real estate agents are more interested in sales than rentals, they can still be a source of resident referrals. Let agents in your area know you have rental property. Be sure to give them a referral fee.

9. Get Help from Other Professionals

Mortgage brokers, lawyers, and accountants you work with can be great resources for resident referrals if they work with your target customers. Be sure to let them know you have rental property and are constantly filling vacancies. Also provide referral fees.

10. Get Help from Service Providers

All service people who work on your rentals are excellent candidates to ask about sharing your flyers or business cards with their customers. Have them write or stamp their names on the flyers or cards before giving them to customers. That way, you know where the referral came from and can reward the right person when one of their customers moves in.

11. Get Help from Insurance Companies

Contact local insurance companies that handle placement of individuals whose homes have been partially or fully destroyed. Often they pay rent for several months in advance (perhaps for the full length of time the rental is needed). Depending on the scarcity of the housing market, insurance companies may pay more than market rent. For them, that's still better than paying to place a family in a hotel for several months.

12. Get Help from the Government

Contact the local housing authority if you're interested in serving low-income residents who receive government subsidies such as Section 8 funding. In certain areas, Section 8 certificates and vouchers are widely available and often the resident's share of the rent can be sent directly to the landlord from a government agency so that the vast majority of the rent is guaranteed. To get started, register your properties with the local housing authority, which is listed in the government section of your telephone directory.

13. Even Your Spouse Can Help!

Always consult your spouse for ideas. He or she could have terrific ideas that you haven't thought of. I get loads of ideas from my wife, Dot, who came up with the idea years ago to go on a cruise at least once a year to learn new marketing and management ideas from other successful landlords and enjoy the fruits of our hard work.

VII. UTILIZE MARKETING TOOLS

Every profession has tools of the trade. Use the following tools to find your ideal residents.

1. Make the Most of Signage

Use a large, professional-looking For Rent sign (18″ × 24″) in the yard. If there is a lot of walk-by or drive-by traffic in front of your rental, use a two-sided For Rent sign right near the sidewalk so everybody that passes cannot help but notice that you have a rental available, coming from either direction.

Also consider using a yard sign such as those used by real estate agents, and attach a rider indicating the number of bedrooms. (The rider can also advertise any other highly attractive features about your rental or attractive terms, such as an option to buy.)

Order For Rent signs from a sign company that can have your phone number actually printed on the sign. Signs on which you have to add your phone number may look just like everyone else's signs in town. If this is the case in your area, a professionally printed/painted sign can help make your place stand out just a bit more, and in some markets, every little bit helps. Plus, with the phone number printed on the signs, no one will be tempted to steal them.

Hold an open house for rentals and put up flags, streamers, or balloons to attract attention. When having an open house, instead of just using one rental sign in the front yard where the open house will take place, arrange to have three or four directional signs leading up to the rental. This is especially effective at busy nearby intersections because as prospects get closer to the property, each sign stimulates more interest. Put a distinctive symbol on each sign that stays constant (e.g., a bird) so you can tell them to follow the signs with the bird.

Whatever you do, make sure it's obvious that you have a vacancy, so when prospects drive by, it's clear the place is for rent. You could also leave flyers describing your rental in a "Take One" box. Or devise an advertising message and have it printed on door hangers or flyers to put on every door near the property. Make sure your phone number is in large, bold type on all your flyers, advertisements, and signs.

2. Make the Most of Your Ads

Use an appealing company name in all your signs and advertising; for example, Majestic Investments, Rainbow Rentals, Premiere Properties, Happy Homes, or Sunshine Investments.

On your classified newspaper ads, start with a short bold headline. Ask the newspaper representative if your headline can be in a slightly larger type than other ads and bold. In most cases, there's no extra charge to do this, but if not, it's worth a few extra dollars to make your ad stand out.

Find out how ads are positioned in the newspaper column. What determines their order? Then construct your ad so that it will appear near the top of its category. For example, if the For Rent ads for each city appear in alphabetical order, start your ad with a word that begins with the letter "A" (A-1 Rental Homes). Having your ad appear close to the top can greatly increase the number of calls you receive from prospective residents.

When you place a display ad in the newspaper, consider putting a dashed border around the entire ad to create the look of a coupon. People respond to coupons.

3. Make the Most of Internet Marketing

Resources on the Internet offer ways to reach residents that are limited only by your imagination. Major Web sites reaching thousands of prospec-

Refer Prospects to Your Web Site

What do you do when people call to inquire about your rental properties? Point them to your Web site where you can fully promote your rentals far better than you can do in any other form of advertising and at very little cost, compared to what other advertising would cost. The key is to include your Web site address on every and all print matter regarding your rentals. If you don't currently have a rental Web site, you can check the Internet to find many companies that will help you create one. Landlords design their Web sites so that prospective residents can learn about their properties. They're complete with pictures of the insides and/or outsides of the homes. Prospects can tour your rental right on their computers without having to disturb the current residents. Some of the rental Web sites also include the criteria for resident selection, a rental application that can be downloaded along with rental policies, and any amenities, services, and community information.

Your residents and others can also refer people to your Web site, including those who don't even live in the area now but are moving to town. One landlord shared how he saved two-thirds of the time he used to spend explaining what his properties offer by referring people to his Web site. When prospects contact him after looking at his Web site, they're ready to rent.

tive residents allow landlords to post available rentals *(e.g., http://www .rent.com or http://www.apartments.com)*. You'll want to advertise your site through one or more of the rental advertising Web sites. The vast majority of the new generation of residents check the Internet as a primary source for finding rental housing. To not advertise on the Web would be unthinkable because you'll miss reaching a large percentage of prospective residents. Access to sites where you can promote your rentals can be found on MrLandlord.com.

4. Make the Most of the Telephone

Use voice mail with a teaser message and your Web site address, if you have one. I also suggest getting Caller ID on your phone. Some prospects may call and not leave a message. However, with Caller ID, you can still discover the phone numbers of all who call, and call them back to see if you can meet their housing needs. For every inquirer you talk to, get contact information, including both work and home phone numbers and an e-mail address, so that you have more than one way to follow up.

5. Make the Most of Handouts and Written Communication

Because many prospects are only concerned about the bottom line and price factors when selecting a rental, you can put together a fact sheet that compares costs of rentals in the area, energy-saving costs on utility bills, savings on gas, or rental discounts that are offered, etc. A handout highlighting all the features and rental extras is great to have

---

The Value of Having Caller ID

Here's the success story of one landlord who said, "Twice I've rented to people who called, got a recorded message, and hung up. What did I do? I called back the number on the Caller ID log and said I was returning their call inquiring about the rental home. I described the place, and then told them to just come and take a look at it to see if they've found their next place to live. They showed up, rented, and remain paid up."

for prospects. It makes sure they see *everything* you have to offer. Rental discounts may sound good, but half of your prospects may be quickly persuaded by having an extra kitchen appliance included in the rental. Descriptive words in your handout, such as *professionally decorated* or *cottage cute,* can add to the property's, appeal, especially to women.

At the top of your flyers and even your rental applications, have these words boldly printed: Our Residents Are Always Number 1. (Yes, consider your rental application one of your strongest marketing tools.) With every written resident communication, use a rubber stamp to add these words: Remember to refer a friend.

VIII. SHOW THE PROPERTY

Use the following ideas as a checklist for effectively showing your property to prospective renters. If qualified applicants are hard to come by, I suggest you do not let prospects inspect your property on their own, because it's human nature to look for reasons *not* to rent. Instead, you should be there to make sure you present the best selling points about the property.

1. Set a Positive Tone before the Showing

When setting up an appointment with a prospect over the phone, be direct in your instructions. State clearly that they can stop looking because you have a residence to meet their needs.

Communicate enthusiasm when talking with prospects over the phone. Even if you use an answering machine, make sure your message is upbeat and informative. The mood you first create with prospects can stimulate interest or, at least, encourage them not to avoid you. Sound positive, and communicate only good features when talking on the phone to all inquires. Smile, smile, smile!

Before concluding a phone conversation with your prospects, tell them to remind you to show them the free gift you give to all new residents who move in this month. However, don't reveal what that gift is over the phone. You want them to remain curious, which doubles the likelihood that they will actually be at the showing.

Have at least two or three prospects interested in seeing the rental meet at the same time to create a sense of competition. If possible, do *not* show the property to just one prospect at a time.

Do you know the most attractive routes for prospects to drive to your rental property? Always give directions that take them past the most attractive sights. Definitely avoid directing them via any nearby eyesores on their first visit to your property.

Before you show prospects your properties, give them a flyer that lists the many features of the rental and your service, and include your contact phone number on it. This helps them take note of the best features of your rental during the showing.

2. Include Signs of Welcome

Place a welcome mat at the entrance of your rentals that you are showing.

If you are scheduled to meet one prospect at your rental for a showing, on the front door of the rental put an inexpensive yet attractive sign that reads: Future Home of _____ (prospect's name). This strategy welcomes your prospect with an immediate and positive impression.

Whenever you're in your vacant rental property putting on the finishing touches, put an "OPEN" sign outside the building. A passerby seeing the sign may knock on the door and give you an opportunity to show the unit while you are there.

Place flowers or potted plants near the front door to increase favorable impressions.

3. Establish Rapport with Your Prospects

Don't rush into your leasing presentation the moment you stand face to face with your prospects. Just asking their names and how they heard about your property does not qualify as establishing rapport. Personalize. Find out interesting things about them. Ask where they work, what they do for a living, what they like to do for fun. Find areas you have in common and use that information to customize your presentation.

Use your prospects' names as often as possible in your conversation. The more you say their names, the more connected and comfortable they'll feel toward you, making it easier for them to accept your rental offer.

Refrain from talking negatively about previous residents when talking to prospective residents. For example, don't use the word *deadbeats* in front of your prospects or your prospects will think you attract that sort of resident. Instead, talk about model residents who you want them to live up to. And if you stay positive in your communication, they will be ten times more likely to call you back—if they don't make the decision to rent from you the same day you show it.

4. Be Sure to Listen Intently to What They Say

The more your prospect talks, the more engaged they are in the selling process. So ask open-ended questions, talk less, listen more, and increase your leasing effectiveness! Describe the benefits of your place compared with where they live.

Find out the answer to this question: Why are you moving? Discover what the prospects are unhappy with in their current living conditions. You'll find out the answer if you establish that rapport previously mentioned. Selling features is a waste of time, so some landlords sell benefits. What about selling solutions? If your prospects have a problem with closet space, your closets may be the solution. Or if their current home is noisy or dark, you might have the perfect quiet, sunny new home for them. Find out what they have a problem with at their current home and solve it for them. Don't worry about all those other features and benefits you may not have to talk about; those will be gravy. Never apologize for anything that you may consider a shortcoming in the rental. Instead, focus solely on the good features. Besides, what seems negative to you may be what your prospects are used to; they may never have thought of it as a problem and may even prefer it. For example, a small kitchen may be preferred for the convenience of everything being within reach and easy to keep clean.

5. Don't Just Give Prices; Sell Value

In this age of heavy competition and concern over high prices, you want to build value as a way to overcome any objections to the rent for which you're asking. Selling value is how you can really stand out from your competitors.

Too many landlords simply list information about the apartments and amenities. But telling a prospect you have a particular number of bedrooms for a certain price is not enough. Take time to talk about the unique features of the rooms, the spacious closets, and so on. Be descriptive for every room you mention. This all helps paint a mental picture of value.

Before you begin showing a property, ask your prospects what particular features they are looking for in their next home (e.g., large closets, big rooms, etc.). If you are able to offer what they are seeking, be sure to take time to emphasize and direct their attention and conversation to these items during the showing.

6. Provide Pertinent and Extra Information

Know the neighborhood, not just the home. Today's renters are savvy, time starved, and solution oriented. Are you prepared to lease to today's renters, or are you still trying to rent to yesterday's renters? Renters today need landlords who know as much about the neighborhood as they do about the rental. How prepared are you?

When applicants come to see your rental, I suggest giving them a sheet with reference information. Making this information available to future residents is an excellent way to demonstrate your helpfulness, credibility, and professionalism, and will significantly increase your leasing performance.

What do I mean by "reference" information? It's the information future residents are most likely to find useful based on questions or objections asked most often. Here are examples of reference information:

- A list of moving companies
- Utilities, cable/satellite TV, and Internet service contacts
- Checklist of things to remember on moving day
- Free places to obtain moving boxes
- Address change forms from the post office
- Information on neighborhood stores, restaurants, auto repair shops, and other services

All this adds to the image that you care to assist them, which helps you win the prospects' favor so that they decide to rent from you instead of your competitors.

7. Help Residents Visualize Moving In

When showing prospective residents certain rooms, ask questions about which pieces of their furniture would go where. For example, "Will your bed fit better on this wall or that wall?" or "Where do you see your living room couch?" As you enter different rooms, also ask what they'd use different rooms for. "Which member of your family will probably use this bedroom? Will it be used as an office or exercise room?" Ask these questions to get prospects to visualize moving in and already living in the property, bringing you one step closer to closing the deal.

8. Sell Yourself—Attitude and Appearance Count

Always assume everyone who contacts you about renting will rent from you. The idea that they might not should not seem possible. When displayed in a positive and courteous manner, your assumptive attitude will produce results. You've got to sincerely believe that the rental you offer is the best value available for the price you charge. If you (or your manager) indeed believe that, then you'll easily convince the first qualified prospect that your property is the best value available.

Even if prospective residents love a property, they may still walk away from the deal if they have doubts about you, the landlord. When you're renting a property, unlike selling a home, you're initiating a long-term relationship. Prospective residents look for a landlord who is professional and knowledgeable. They may ask how they can reach you for repairs or in an emergency. You appear more competent if you can answer such questions easily. It will become more critical to understand how all aspects of marketing help attract and retain residents. Both the condition of the property and the competence of the landlord/salesperson are vital to marketing.

When meeting with prospects, be sure your appearance is neat and you're well groomed. In my experience, your attire could make the difference of whether someone decides to rent from you or not. Come across as warm and caring when showing your homes. Be enthusiastic and accentuate the positive aspects of your rental. Enthusiasm is contagious. (Beware: Lack of enthusiasm is contagious, too.) Don't be the biggest obstacle to filling your vacancies.

9. Do Things in a Memorable Way

To make an impression, you could have a big gift-wrapped box sitting on the floor in the first room a prospect enters. When asked about it, say it's the move-in gift that goes to the first qualified applicant to fill out the application. Or, place an easel in the front room holding a white board with these words printed on it: This Month's Special. Then write down special incentive gifts or discounts you're offering for those who sign up today (e.g., gift certificate for dinner for two).

10. What to Do At the End of the Showing

When you finish showing your rental to prospects, instead of asking, "What do you think?" ask "Would you prefer our standard, custom, or deluxe home package." If someone turns down your rental, always seek

Give a Child Extra Attention

When planning to show a rental to a qualified prospect, along with getting the rental in the usual rent-ready condition, add one special item in the bedroom that will probably be used by a child. That special item could be a large, inexpensive, but colorful toy box. Always invite prospects to bring all members of their family to the showing. During the rental showing, make a special stop in the bedroom with the toy box. Invite any younger person present to come over to the box and tell him/her to choose any toy as a surprise gift. Designate an area of the room or house as a play area, and allow the child to play with the toy while you show the rental to the parents and have them fill out the application. Now comes the clincher. After the child picks the toy of choice, tell him or her, "If your parents like the home and decide to move in, you get to have the entire toy box."

to find out the real reason so you can adjust your marketing plan or rental preparation.

Offer a move-in gift as an incentive to close the deal (e.g., a DVD player or microwave oven for the first qualified applicant who fills out an application). This is also referred to as a "Look and Lease Now" option to help create urgency. Offer an additional incentive to lease within 24 hours of the first contact with the property. Some landlords successfully offer an additional $100 off the first month—or a computer. Note: Whatever you offer to one, you need to offer to all.

IX. FOLLOW UP

Completing the following activities after the initial phone call or showing can make the difference between renting the property or not. It also shows prospects they're working with a professional.

1. Get contact information from everyone who calls and expresses interest. Everyone who contacts you may not make it to the showing appointment and everyone who does come may not make a decision at first look. By having phone numbers, you can systematically follow up with those who express interest in your property. Most landlords give no further thought to prospects who don't show up or don't make quick decisions at the time of showing. However, smart landlords know that by simply calling them back, they may still have a chance of renting to them.

2. Ask for the e-mail address of each future resident either by telephone or when they arrive to see the property. This becomes another way to be in touch with each future resident at no cost—compared to the cost of a traditional mail approach. Imagine the marketing power of sending free e-mail newsletters to dozens of future residents who had visited your rentals in the past year.

3. Don't delay selecting from possible applicants. Sign up the first qualified applicant who meets your criteria. Don't simply wait to collect a large number of applicants to choose the best. You'll lose good people and valuable time.

4. If you have more than one qualified applicant and only one rental, give the second applicant a letter or certificate saying that

he/she has been preapproved for any of your rentals as soon as another becomes available. Give a discount if he or she brings that letter or certificate back when checking with you over the next weeks or months.

CHECKLIST

How well do you learn from mistakes—yours and others? Watch out for these:

✓ **Not trying different strategies.** Some landlords only know one or two ways to advertise, so they don't do enough to get their places rented fast. Use many different methods to fill your vacancy. Reread this book for lots of ideas.

✓ **Eliminating marketing efforts when times get tough.** When cash flow slows down, you may be tempted to stop your marketing efforts. But if you cut these, you eliminate the very activity that brings in new customers! Don't cut your marketing efforts; instead, analyze them and direct them more effectively.

✓ **Not measuring results.** Don't wait until times get tight to start measuring your marketing results. By constantly analyzing them, you can reinvest in what's working and drop what's not working.

✓ **Putting all your advertising dollars in one area.** Diversifying your efforts will increase the frequency and reach of your messages and stretch your investment. It's easy to get hooked into advertising with a local newspaper and put the majority of your dollars there.

✓ **Not keeping your present residents happy.** No need to keep bringing residents in the front door if you keep losing them out the back door. Their satisfaction will keep your properties filled. See Step 9 for dozens of strategies on how to keep residents longer.

5

SCREEN OUT
PROBLEM RESIDENTS

"It's better to have no residents, than to accept a bad resident."
—JEFFREY TAYLOR

After using the action steps and marketing strategies in Step 4, your phone will start ringing. Now it's vital that you know how to screen and select residents who are qualified. This step gives you a simple screening process, including ways to avoid renting to residents most likely to generate problems.

I. SET UP SCREENING AND SELECTION PROCEDURES

When evaluating prospective residents and analyzing these categories, be concerned with the applicants' payment history, stability history, and headache history. I suggest following this five-step process:

1. Collect an application and processing fee from each applicant.
2. Do an initial review, verify information, and score a New Resident Criteria Checklist based on answers.
3. Obtain a credit check and eviction report on all applicants who pass initial review or achieve a minimum score.
4. Inspect the applicant's current residence and run a criminal background check.

5. Select the first applicant who satisfactorily meets your minimum criteria and completes the screening process. Immediately request required rent and deposit.

1. Collect an Application and Processing Fee from Each Applicant

Charge an application fee (or credit check fee) to cover the cost of the credit check you require. (In the United States, the average application fee charged by a landlord is $20 to $25. Check your state laws for any limitations.) Although some landlords make the application fee nonrefundable, I tell prospects I'll apply this fee toward their move-in costs if their credit check meets my minimum criteria. That way, they don't resist paying it.

Paying that fee starts the screening process and indicates that your prospects aren't just "kicking tires" and wasting time. When receiving an application, ask for the applicant's driver's license to ensure the person's identity. If more than one applicant applies, collect an application and fee from each adult applicant—even if they're husband and wife. Treat them as you would if they applied as nonmarried roommates.

Ripping Off Landlords for Years

Nick Koon was a highly successful real estate investor from Ohio and a mentor of mine. Nick shared with me what happened when he asked for a $20 screening fee after a young man had filled out one of his applications. The man obliged and gave him a $20 bill. Nick then asked to see his driver's license to verify his identify. The young man started laughing and said, "I've been ripping landlords off for years and you're the first one who's asked to see my driver's license. Can I have my $20 back?" Nick responded, "Son, that $20 was my screening fee and you've been screened."

2. Do an Initial Review, Verify Information, and Score a New Resident Criteria Checklist Based on Answers

Similar to what banks and loan companies use when extending credit, I have a point system for evaluating prospects based on 20 to 25 criteria. Applicants receive points each time they meet a screening criteria. Once they accumulate so many points, they objectively qualify to rent my place. Using this point system allows me to be consistent in how I evaluate every applicant in the three main screening categories—payment history, stability history, and headache history.

Payment history. If the applicant doesn't have a history of paying on time, you can expect history to repeat itself.

What is the applicant's payment history and how much is the applicant currently paying for housing? If the amount the applicant will be paying is more than 25 percent higher than the current housing payment, be concerned. The applicant may not be able to handle this "jump" financially. Check with the applicant's current landlord to find out if payments have historically been made on time. Beware that some landlords may be less than truthful when answering questions because they want to get rid of problem residents or hinder good residents from moving. That's why it's important to request at least two former addresses on the application; former landlords have nothing to lose by answering questions honestly.

What are the applicant's current monthly expenses? When landlords screen applicants, they often look at income but rarely at expenses. Your concern is not only how well the applicant has been paying rent, but also the number and dollar amount of other current bills. Ask the applicant to list expenses on the application, then plug total expenses and income into a landlord calculator. Use it to calculate how much the applicant can afford to spend on rent. (You can find a landlord calculator and other helpful calculators for investors at MrLandlord.com.)

What are the names of personal references and contacts for emergency assistance? These contacts become your backup for collecting delinquent rent, if necessary. People who pose low financial risk have friends or

My Definition of an Emergency

On my rental applications, I have changed a standard statement from "Please provide the name of an emergency contact" to "In the event of some emergency that would prevent you from paying rent, please provide the name of at least one person or agency who could be called on for assistance." This clearly presents *my* definition of an emergency, which is an inability to pay rent. I verify the information by calling the contacts and saying, "Mrs. Smith, you were listed as an emergency contact by Mr. Jones as someone who could help him if he was unable to pay the rent. I am calling to verify this." You'd be surprised at some of the responses! "No, I'm not paying that turkey's rent! Who gave you that idea?"

Though it's not fail-safe, this system greatly increases the chances of collecting money. I've found that qualified residents come up with qualified emergency contacts. If they tell me up front they'd assist their nephew, coworker, employee, or fellow church member, then the chances of doing so are greater when a problem occurs.

family members willing to at least say they'd help the applicant financially. When you call the personal references, of course they'll say good things. But the real purpose for talking with them is to get their help if your resident skips out. Find out up front if they'd be willing cover rent. If they say yes, I may then ask if they would serve as a cosigner on the lease.

3. Obtain a Credit Check and Eviction Report on All Applicants Who Pass Initial Review or Achieve a Minimum Score

When I do an initial review of the application and add up points, if I don't see enough points in the applicant's favor (or there are glaring negative points), the process ends here. However, if everything else about the applicant adds up, I obtain a credit report. Similarly, be sure your application includes a statement indicating that the applicant authorizes you to obtain this report. Use the credit report to expose or verify the applicant's address and residency dates over the past seven years. It also helps identify and give points to individuals who have stable rental histories.

Additional points are given if the applicant has the following:

- A sufficient amount of monthly income (equal to three times the amount of rent)
- A verifiable source of income
- The ability to pay the full deposit and rent requested
- A checking account
- No late notices reported from the current landlord
- A credit report score that is above the minimum score that you determine

Stable history. You want residents who have verifiable, long-term rental histories with good payment records.

Avoid transient residents. Applicants who are transient have no bank account or stable running job or source of income (one year minimum), and have a record of moving often in the past three years.

A *Verification* **T**ip

Applicants sometimes list a friend as the landlord or employer. That friend is poised to respond positively to questions regarding the applicant. The person responding may, in fact, be the true landlord but not truthful in responding to questions. Therefore, I suggest first asking a question to which the person must know the correct answer. For example, if an applicant stated his current rent as $650, I would ask, "Is the applicant currently paying $750 a month?" If the person says yes, I know I'm not being told the truth and/or that person isn't the real landlord. I simply say thank you and hang up. I suggest you don't go through all your questions until you are speaking with someone who can give you straight answers.

Add points for good rental history. Using my point system, I add points to applicants who have demonstrated stability in their rental and/or employment histories. I ask applicants to give their last two addresses and dates of residency, then I give 1, 2, or 3 points corresponding to the number of verifiable years each person has stayed at the residence (less than one year earns 0 points; one year earns 1 point, etc.). If they didn't have responsibility for paying rent at their former addresses (e.g., living with relatives), they get 0 points.

Add points for income stability. I ask applicants for their past two places of employment or sources of income, then1 I give 1, 2, or 3 points corresponding to the number of verifiable years each person had the same employer or source of income (one source of income for less than one year earns 0 points; same source of income for one year earns 1 point, etc.).

Other points include:

- No prior evictions
- Verification from employer or income provider that income should continue for the next year or foreseeable future
- No past notices from previous landlord regarding upkeep violations
- Can get utility service at your property in their own name
- No community standard violations, health violations, or safety violations at current residence

Headache history. When the average landlord looks at rental applicants, most are concerned about payment history and ability to pay the rent. If the applicant appears qualified enough to afford the rent, that's good enough for them.

But determining if someone can pay me is only *one* factor. Remember, many investors don't last long as rental property owners because they experience headaches and get tired of dealing with problems that arise. Some don't hold on to properties long term because they want to avoid landlording challenges.

But I know that a large percentage of headaches can be avoided if the screening procedure analyzed *more* than ability to pay rent. You can learn to identify applicants who have a history of creating headaches in areas beyond not paying rent. In fact, nonpayment of rent is easily dealt with legally compared to other problems that cause headaches. Wouldn't your life be more stress-free if you screened out residents already known for causing headaches?

You may ask, Why not just ask the current landlord if the person caused problems or headaches? I wish it were easy to get a straight answer. Many landlords hope you'll relieve them of their "headaches." But if you ask applicants the following questions, you'll quickly tell if they need "careful" screening.

Have you had reoccurring problems with the property at your last home or apartment? It's amazing how the same problems follow residents from property to property. For example, if residents have recurring problems with their toilets in their current homes, before long that same problem will occur at your rental. If you discover this problem during the screening process, you'll avoid getting headaches later. Do you turn applicants down because they say they've had recurring toilet problems? No, but when I hear this response, the antenna on my head goes up high. I continue screening cautiously while sirens inside are blaring "red alert."

Have you had disagreements with your last manager or landlord? If they've had disagreements with previous managers, they likely aren't bashful to tell you about their "problem landlord." In fact, residents who cause the most headaches—those who always have "drama" in their lives—enjoy talking about the problems "others" have caused.

In a nonthreatening, conversational manner, I let applicants talk openly. After all, I've introduced myself as the assistant property manager ready to help them out. If I'm not seen as the owner, they're less likely to have their guard up and more likely to talk about previous problems. The more they "badmouth" a current or former landlord, the more the "red-alert" sirens blare inside my head. As a result, I look for objective reasons for *not* renting to them.

What is the name of your attorney? (This is asked in the application under "Names of professional references.") If applicants are able to fill out this part, proceed with caution.

Are there negative marks in your credit history that I'll discover when I run your credit report? The response to that question is vital because a dishonest person poses an extremely high risk. Examine all information on the application and compare responses submitted with information noted on the credit report. Discrepancies give you reason to doubt.

Have you been late on a rent payment in the past three years? It's been my experience that many residents pay late at least once in a three-year period. Being late once or twice isn't the major issue; it's the follow-up question and response that may break the deal. Ask, "What was the reason for the late payment?" What excuses do they give? Who do they blame? The more excuses I hear, the more I know they have a history of creating headaches.

Using these questions to screen applicants can save you thousands of dollars and tons of headaches. Remember, your long-term happiness as a real estate investor is a direct result of how well you avoid bringing in problem residents.

Other factors help determine an applicant's potential cooperation level. I also consider if the applicant

- is on time for the showing appointment,
- fills out an application completely,
- has no pets (if you have a no-pet policy),
- converses in a courteous, nonargumentative manner with no profanity,
- has no neighbor complaints or police reports on file at previous addresses, and
- has no criminal history.

The Importance of Credit Checks

Some landlords don't obtain credit reports on low-income applicants. They assume negative marks will come back. However, another reason to run the report is to compare what it includes against what applicants have told you. You want to verify their honesty.

It's one thing to have marginal credit; it's another to lie about it. As a landlord, I don't expect to attract "perfect" residents. After all, if they had excellent credit, they'd likely be buying, not renting. I can work with applicants who have less-than-perfect credit reports; I prefer *not* to work with applicants who lack integrity.

4. Inspect the Applicant's Current Residence and Run a Criminal Background Check

If you can, visit an applicant's current residence to see how that person would take care of your property. Six months from now, your property will look just like their current residence. If you're not happy with what you see, don't rent to the applicant based on objective reasons like community standard violations, health violations, or safety violations found on the property. If you are considering renting to a pet owner, see if you detect any odor in the premises or damage to the furniture while viewing the property. If you do accept a pet, I would suggest that any cats and dogs must be spayed or neutered and must be up to date on all shots! Require an additional $250 deposit/fee, which will be partially used to clean the unit per the allergy needs of prospective allergic tenants. One additional note on furniture: When people have high-quality furniture and bring it into a rental home, they're more likely to be stable and less likely to move out in the middle of the night.

If you received permission on the application to run a criminal background check, and the prospect has made it this far along in the screening process, now is the time to perform it.

5. Select the First Applicant Who Satisfactorily Meets Your Minimum Criteria and Completes the Screening Process. Immediately Request Required Rent and Deposit

Contact the selected applicant. When applicants first apply, let them know you'll contact them within 24 to 48 hours if they are accepted. Because credit checks and eviction reports can be done instantly online, you can process an application quickly. If verifying information with previous landlords or employers takes longer, tell them you're waiting for responses and ask for assistance with those responses.

Send a credit denial letter. If applicants are turned down because of information on their credit report, you're required to send them a credit denial letter. Denying housing based on reasons other than credit report information doesn't require a written response, though out of courtesy, I suggest sending a note to all applicants, giving them the opportunity to check back in the future. (Refer to the Denial Form in the Appendix.)

Arrange to meet your selected applicant and collect funds needed for move-in (first month's rent and security deposit). If move-in doesn't happen immediately, call the deposit a "holding" deposit until the move-in date. Use these terms to clearly communicate that the purpose of the fee is to "hold" the property exclusively for that applicant, and it gets forfeited if they change their mind. At move-in, it converts to part of or all of a security deposit and falls under all laws related to security deposits.

Only accept certified funds or funds termed "good" before allowing residents to move in. Many landlords have taken checks that later bounced, then found out they were "stuck" with undesirable residents. Their only recourse was starting a legal eviction procedure that could take one to three months to get the residents out—without receiving rent in the interim. If you accept a check from an applicant, either cash it immediately at the applicant's bank or make sure it clears before handing over the keys.

Never accept an applicant without following your complete screening process and policies. You need to have more than good chemistry or a good "gut" feeling. Just one bad resident can create financial and emotional nightmares. Believe me, it's not worth the risk.

6

CONDUCT NEW RESIDENT ORIENTATION

"The easiest time to evict people is before they move in."
—JEFFREY TAYLOR

Without a doubt, certain challenges will arise in the rental business. I've discovered, however, if you identify what those challenges are and address them with your residents before they occur, you'll dramatically reduce the chances of those challenges occurring and definitely reduce the number of times you will have to deal with them. This is what I call "preventive communication." If only I'd had someone to tell me when I started out as a real estate investor what challenges I'd likely encounter and how to avoid or handle them. It sure would have made my first few years less frustrating. So I've identified eight problematic rental areas and stressed how to communicate them to residents in your rental agreement. I encourage you to actually set aside time with your residents before they move in and conduct a new resident orientation. This orientation will give you the opportunity to perform preventive communication to reduce the chances of these problems occurring.

I. ADDRESS POTENTIAL PROBLEMS BEFORE THEY OCCUR

During the new resident orientation, I recommend going over each issue with residents in a businesslike manner before having them sign the rental agreement. This helps start the relationship in agreement, with complete understanding, and in a win-win way. Understand that merely including the sample clauses suggested in this guide is *not* the point. (Have your attorney review any clauses that you use in your agreement whether obtained from here or elsewhere.) What's important is thinking these issues through and communicating them to your residents. Don't be like many real estate investors who get burned out or frustrated because they don't cover certain points until *after* problems occurred. Take time to address key issues and agree on how you'll work together. If you can't come to a mutual understanding, the easiest time to part ways is *before* the relationship starts.

II. CONDUCT A WALK-THROUGH WITH A PROPERTY CONDITION CHECKLIST

Before looking at other issues with your residents, introduce an important rental form at the time of orientation: the property condition checklist (also called a move-in or inventory checklist). Using this form helps make sure you begin the relationship with mutual understanding.

This checklist establishes the condition of the property before move-in so when residents move out, they know in what condition to "return" the property. They will be aware up front what they need to do to be entitled to the return of their full deposit and/or not be held liable for damages that weren't present and noted on the checklist. It also makes sure the landlord and the residents agree about a satisfactory condition at move-in. Anything that is not satisfactory should be noted on the checklist so residents won't be held liable for returning the property in an unsatisfactory condition. This also gives the landlord the opportunity to inform residents in writing of improvements planned.

Make sure the checklist is detailed and categorized according to room. On the form, mark and explain anything that's not satisfactory (e.g., stain on carpet in second bedroom or hot water faucet in bathroom not working). Any later corrections should be noted on this checklist, too.

I suggest having the property in excellent condition with everything in working order when new residents are ready to move in. In fact, it's an absolute must if you want to create a long-term, win-win relationship with them.

During the orientation, you'd conduct a walk-through of the property with checklist in hand. After the walk-through, have residents sign off on the checklist confirming everything is satisfactory. Give them a copy and keep a copy with your records. (See a sample property condition checklist in the Appendix.)

The orientation is also an excellent opportunity to show residents any cut-off switches and discuss how minor upkeep and preventive maintenance will need to be handled. Do not assume residents will know how to properly care for your property.

III. INTRODUCE WIN-WIN, MONEYMAKING MANAGEMENT POLICIES

In this guide, I've continued to use the terms *win-win* and *people-centered management*. These are more than cute-sounding phrases. As part of your management practices, I encourage you to sincerely offer options and incentives that benefit your residents in exchange for their cooperating with your management policies. Start your discussion of issues and policies during your new resident orientation highlighting the following policies that form the foundation for a win-win relationship.

These eight policies are the same moneymaking management policies that I share at seminars and that have helped tens of thousands of rental owners increase their net income and improve residents' performance. When implemented, they can totally change the way you work together—even changing average residents into cooperative, top-performing ones. (Let me share the wording I put in rental agreements to incorporate these policies, noting what you want to address with residents during the new resident orientation. For further discussion on these ideas, read the steps regarding maximizing your cash flow and keeping residents longer.)

Here are eight of the most popular Mr. Landlord win-win, moneymaking management concepts that have helped thousands of owners increase their net rental income and improve the performance of their residents:

1. Custom Home Package
2. Free Upgrade Referral Program
3. 3-Star Resident Loyalty Program

4. Biweekly Payday Rent Payment Plan
5. Worry-Free Payment Methods
6. Future Homebuyers Program
7. Maintenance Guarantee
8. Build Your Creditworthiness Program

Because your agreement is the key contractual document that you and your residents refer to as the foundation for your relationship, it's vital to integrate these concepts and programs into your rental agreement.

1. Custom Home Package

The following resident(s) _____ agree to rent from the owner(s) _____, the premises located at _____.

The premises include the following amenities: (List selected *options* beyond four walls and a floor that resident desires as part of upgraded customized rental price; e.g., choice of wall color in one room, ceiling fans added, computer, washer and dryer, extra phone jack, etc.)

The rental of the premises also includes: (State additional optional rental *space,* such as garage, storage area, yard, parking, or shed, that isn't part of the standard rental price.)

RESIDENT'S RESPONSIBILITY FOR UPGRADE: As part of the 3-Star Resident program, we are pleased to let you know that the following item(s) _____, which is one or more of the upgrades in your custom home package, will become your property after _____ years. Because the item(s) is becoming your property, unless otherwise stated in your agreement, you're responsible for routine maintenance and/or repair of the item(s).

2. Free Upgrade Referral Program

The owner agrees to offer a free property upgrade once a year to any resident who recommends and refers one qualified prospective resident to one of our rentals during the course of any year. For current residents to qualify for the free property upgrade, any referred prospective resident must

1. fill out a rental application,
2. meet the minimum resident criteria, and
3. move in to one of the owner's vacant rentals paying all required funds.

3. 3-Star Resident Loyalty Program

The rental will begin on _____ (date) and continue on a month-to-month basis. Either party may terminate the tenancy or offer to upgrade the terms by giving the other party _____ days written notice. As part of our 3-Star Resident Loyalty Program, we, the owners and managers, look forward to serving your housing and related needs for the next three years until the following date: _____.

During the next three years, you will receive the following benefits as a resident in good rental standing:

- On your first anniversary date, you are entitled to your choice of the following: _____, _____, _____.

- On your second and third anniversary dates, you will again receive your choice of upgrades.

4. Biweekly Payday Rent Payment Plan

Residents have option to pay the owner monthly rent of $_____, payable in advance on or before the first day of each month. Or, if residents prefer and consider it more convenient, residents may elect to have a biweekly agreement (instead of monthly) and pay biweekly (every two weeks to coincide with their payday) rent of $_____, payable in advance the _____ day of every other week. Exception to the due date is when that day falls on a legal holiday, in which case rent is due the next business day.

Note: It's suggested that the biweekly amount be equivalent to 3 to 5 percent higher than the normal monthly rent rate divided in half. For example, if the monthly rate is $800, 5 percent higher would be $840. The biweekly rent amount would be half that total or $420.

5. Worry-Free Payment Methods

Residents may select one of the following worry-free payment methods for paying rent during the rental term, so they don't have to worry about late charges every month. Residents agree by signing this agreement to give permission and authorization to arrange for rent collection by method selected and debit appropriate account(s).

Preferred Method of Payment Selected:

___ Electronic debit from checking or savings account on agreed days or dates each month.
___ Credit or debit card debit from following account: _____
___ Payroll deduction sent directly from employer biweekly or monthly.
___ Other traditional method of payments made by check or money order delivered to designated address may be selected, requiring a handling fee of $_____ per transaction.

6. Future Homebuyers Program, Part I (Regarding On-Time Payments)

The owner has established a Future Homebuyers fund for residents. Residents understand and agree that, following each on-time payment received, owner has agreed to increase the amount of money in the fund by $_____. Residents will be entitled to receive credit for the money accumulated in the fund that can be applied toward purchase of a house at time of closing. The total amount will be referred to as the Future Homebuyers account during the term of the rental.

Residents will be able to receive a credit at closing equal to the amount in their Future Homebuyers account once they have been residents for a minimum of _____ years. Money equivalent to Future Homebuyers account is to be used solely for the purchase of a house and is credited or paid out at time of real estate closing.

The house that residents may purchase and apply the Future Homebuyers account toward can be selected from either the same residence in this agreement or another house offered by the owner or by one of the following real estate brokers or builders:

_____

_____

Please note that the money total increases each month with every on-time payment received by the following due date: _____. If, however, payment is received late, the money total accrued into the Future Homebuyers account up to that point becomes null and void. The account starts accumulating again with the next on-time rental payment.

Future Homebuyers Program, Part 2 (Regarding Property Maintenance and Inspections)

Residents further understand and agree that residents who are

1. responsible for and handle all minor repairs in their residence, and
2. pass semi-annual property inspections will receive an additional voucher of $ _____ toward their Future Homebuyers account each year.

Two property inspections are conducted yearly with a checklist provided to residents in advance of inspections. Failure to handle minor upkeep or repairs or to pass a property inspection nullifies the total amount accumulated up to that point in the resident's Future Homebuyers account.

7. Maintenance Guarantee

The resident understands and agrees that the following major repairs are the responsibility of the owners and managers:

The owners/managers agree to guarantee that these major repairs will be fixed within 72 hours after notification of the problem to owner/manager and acknowledgment of that notification. The resident understands that if one of these stated major repairs is not corrected within 72 hours after notification, the resident will receive *free rent* on a prorated basis starting the fourth day after the day of notification until the problem is corrected.

In addition, it's understood that the Maintenance Guarantee will not be honored if the maintenance problem was caused because of the resident's negligence, abuse, or fault. The resident also agrees that in order for the owner to honor the guarantee, the owner or manager must be given access into the building, with resident's permission, to correct the problem.

Free rent will be awarded in the form of a cash rent rebate on a pro-rated basis, following the next on-time rent received.

8. Build Your Credit Worthiness Program

Residents understand that they will be held accountable for their rental performance while residing in the property. Nonpayment of rent and any outstanding debts are reported to all three major credit bureaus. Any violation of the rental agreement will also be kept in the resident's file. Having a good performance record can have positive benefits that help residents prove creditworthiness with future landlords, creditors, lenders, or mortgage companies.

A review of each resident's performance is done annually and the owner will provide a *good* performance report that will be put into the resident's file and a copy given to all residents who pay on time and follow *all* terms of the rental agreement. Building creditworthiness and good references will help residents participating in the Future Homebuyers Program.

While a copy of the report is provided to residents for records that can be used with future landlords, loan officers, and creditors, please note: Rental violations placed in a resident's file can hurt a resident's creditworthiness and will be made available to future landlords, banks, mortgage companies, and other creditors who they may want to do business with in the future. Therefore, it's important to understand that the performance reports residents establish during the rental term (good or bad) will be with them for many years.

Because of the importance of performances reported, residents will always be notified when a rental violation needs to be corrected and be given the opportunity to immediately do so before it goes in their records, jeopardizing future purchases or renting other homes or apartments.

IV. PERFORM PREVENTIVE COMMUNICATION—CLAUSES ADDRESSING COMMON PROBLEMS

How can you address problematic issues in your rental agreement to help prevent or reduce common management problems from occurring? Include them in your rental agreement so a clear understanding exists between both parties up front and avoid the misunderstandings that often ignite between landlords and residents. Use the resident orientation to cover these issues and sample clauses to clearly communicate with new and renewing residents concerning what each party is responsible for in the rental relationship.

As with the win-win management policies previously discussed, it's vital that you take time to think through how to handle these key issues and discuss them with your residents in advance. Don't get burned out or frustrated because you didn't cover certain issues until *after* problems occurred. Never expect anyone to cooperate the way you want them to—unless you take time to tell them what you expect.

You'll find a sample rental agreement in the Appendix to use as a starting point. Again, I strongly suggest you join a local real estate association and obtain a rental agreement provided by the association because it likely includes legally required clauses for your state. If there's not an association near you, go to MrLandlord.com and request state-specific rental forms. Note: In some states, if certain language isn't included in your agreement, the entire document may not be enforceable.

V. SCHEDULE CONTINUING RESIDENT ORIENTATION

If you already have residents, I'd suggest that on their anniversary dates you conduct a "continuing resident orientation" to introduce your win-win management policies and discuss the issues below. Also on a resident's anniversary date, update your rental agreement and incorporate some of the wording noted here. Use the points as a checklist to review your rental agreement and see if you've addressed all the various rental situations outlined.

When developing, reviewing, or modifying your rental agreement, add clauses to address issues highlighted and have your agreement reviewed by an attorney to ensure it meets your state's requirements.

Trust me. By addressing the following ten issues with your new and continuing residents, both verbally and in your rental agreement, you'll save yourself tons of future frustration:

1. Occupants' use of premises/utilities
2. Payments, deposits, and cosigners
3. Charges, fees, and options
4. Noncompliance, house rules, and lease violations
5. Maintenance, repairs, and emergencies
6. Pets and vehicles
7. Alterations, upkeep, and improvements
8. Damages, liabilities, and insurance
9. Renewals and move-outs
10. Correspondence, acceptance, and agreement

I. Occupants' Use of Premises/Utilities

Limited occupancy. Residents understand that only the following person(s) _____ listed in this rental agreement is/are permitted to occupy the dwelling. Additional occupants, including short-term visits by relatives or friends, may not exceed seven days without permission from the owner, or be subject to either termination of this agreement or an additional charge of $_____ per month.

Residential use. Residents agree to only use the dwelling for residential purposes and not to conduct any business activity or store any materials on the property or within the dwelling that relates to anything commercial or to a hobby that is not consistent with residential standards.

Nonassignment/subletting of rental agreement. Residents agree not to assign this agreement, or to sublet any part of the property, or to allow any other person to live therein other than those listed in this agreement without first requesting permission from the landlord and paying an appropriate surcharge.

Utilities. Residents agree to place the following utilities (_____, _____, _____) in their name before moving into the premises and to be responsible for payments. Residents agree to be responsible for all said utilities through the duration of their occupancy and further agree to authorize the landlord to charge additional rent or to deduct the amount from the deposit for any unpaid bills.

Appliances not included. Residents understand that appliances of any kind are not part of the rented property and are not included in the rental price. If any are remaining when residents move in, at residents' option, they may purchase them from the landlord for $_____. The landlord is not responsible for replacement or repair. If residents should ever decide that they don't want them, the landlord will take them back for $_____ if left clean and in working order when residents move. The landlord will remove any appliances at residents' request.

Additional appliances. No additional appliances, including air conditioners, washing machines, clothes dryers, or other major appliances are to be installed without owner's written permission. If additional appliances are added, there will be an additional minimum charge of $_____ per month. In addition, unless otherwise stated in this agreement, if permission is given to add any appliance, residents may be required to pay at their own expense for installation of separate electrical or plumbing lines or other installation-related expenses.

2. Payments, Deposits, and Cosigners

Pay in full. Residents agree to pay on time and in full or be evicted. Time is of the essence for payment of rent and strict compliance with the lease due dates is required. The eviction process begins on the ____ day of the month if rent payment has not been received by the following due date: _____. Eviction proceedings will begin promptly.

Discounted rent. The discounted rental price is $_____ per month. When paid after the _____, the normal rent of $ _____ is due. (Note: Some states do not permit "discounted rent" clauses but permit late charges.)

Late charge. Residents agree to pay late charge of $ _____ for payment not received by the _____ of the month. All payments lost in the mail will be considered unpaid until received by owner or manager. Residents acknowledge that if two or more late payments are noted within any 12-month period, it is probable that the rental agreement may not be renewed.

Method of payment. Rent must be paid in full with one check, money order, or cashier's check, or by automatic bank draft, electronic funds transfer (EFT), or debit. The landlord hereby designates the method of payment to be the following: _____.
Note: If payment by check is permitted, and any payment to the landlord is ever not honored or returned from the bank (regardless of reason), residents must pay all future rent as follows: _____.

Payments by mail. Rent may be mailed through the U.S. Postal Service at residents' risk to: _____.
Any rents lost in the mail will be treated as if unpaid until received by owner. Rent must be in the owner's possession by the due date. Prior experience indicates that rents should be mailed well in advance of due date. However, because the owner is not responsible for any delays due to the mail or delivery service, even if the rent payment was postmarked before the due date, if we have not yet received the payment by the due date, residents will lose any discount or be subject to late fees.

Mail fraud protection. All rent checks or other payments due from residents must say on the back "For Deposit Only."

Resident reimbursements. Expenses are never to be deducted from the rent. Rent is to be paid in full and on time. Rent rebates, expenses, and reimbursements are always to be handled as separate transactions.

Partial payment. The acceptance by management of partial payments of rent due will not under any circumstances constitute a waiver of the landlord nor affect any notice or legal proceedings in unlawful detainer theretofore given or commenced.

Allocation of payments. All money received from residents is first applied to any past due balance on resident's account, including unpaid rent, charges, fees, deposits, damages, or utility charges. Second, the balance of money received is then applied to current rent due.

Nonauthorized collection. If any payments are made in person or directly to management personnel, residents understand that they will always receive a company-approved receipt for payment. Residents further understand that it is not normal practice for anyone to come to the rental to collect rents, and residents further understand they are always to receive a company-approved receipt with payments made in person. Residents understand that any payment without the designated receipt given or to unauthorized personnel will not be credited to residents' account.

Security deposit. The security deposit is to be applied to remedy any default by residents in performance of residents' obligations under the lease and to repair damages to the premises caused by residents, not including ordinary wear and tear. Within ____ days after delivery of possession of the leased premises back to the owner or manager, the deposit shall be refunded to residents or an accounting of deposit expenditures shall be given to residents. If costs or repairing damages exceed the amount of the deposit, residents shall be responsible for all such excess costs. Residents may not at any time apply the deposit to be used as last month's rent or for any other sum due under this agreement.

3. Charges, Fees, and Options

Collection fee. A $25 service fee is charged to residents if the landlord must pick up the rent.

Notice delivery fee. Residents agree to pay the landlord a delivery or service charge of $_____ if it is necessary to deliver a notice to this address to notify of a violation of the rental agreement (for example, a pay or quit notice is delivered and/or posted on the _____ day of the month if rent has not been received).

Returned checks. All returned checks will be charged a $_____ bad check fee, and lose any discount for early payment. After giving one bad check, residents agree to make all future payments by money order or cashier's check for a minimum period of ___ months.

Attorney fees. If payment is not made by the ___ day of the month, an attorney will be contacted to initiate eviction proceedings. Attorney's fee of _____ will be added to the amount due once eviction proceedings are initiated. Regarding any legal proceedings, the losing party agrees to pay all attorney and court costs needed to enforce this rental agreement to the prevailing party in a court decision.

Lockout fees. Should residents lock themselves out of dwelling and be unable to gain access, they should call the landlord to let them in. The landlord service fee for this during business hours of _____ to _____ is $_____. After hours, holidays, and weekends, the fee is $_____. The fee is due and payable at the time of service.

4. Noncompliance, House Rules, and Lease Violations

Financial hardship. Because unforeseen circumstances may occur during the rental term and create difficulty for residents to make timely rent payments, residents agree to permit direct contact from the owner with the following individuals, companies, or organizations for assistance in past due rental payments: _____.

Report to credit bureaus. Residents authorize the owner to inform local and national credit agencies of their good or bad credit performance with regard to rental payment. Failure to pay rent will be reported to the three national credit bureaus and be put on residents' credit history.

Lease violation. If residents violate any provision in the lease agreement, the landlord has the right to begin eviction procedures and terminate this agreement.

Condo/homeowners association rules. If there are condominium or other association rules and regulations governing the premises, residents agree to conform to them.

Outside fires. The use of any gas or charcoal grill or outside fires of any kind is not permitted anywhere at any time on the premises without the prior written approval of management.

Noise/language. Residents agree not to make noise or a disturbance that interferes with the peaceful enjoyment of the premises for all residents and neighbors. Residents further agree not to use profane language in common areas or around the premises. If police are called to the rental home for resident-related problems/disturbance, residents are subject to eviction.

Exterior fixtures/signs. Residents agree not to attach outside antennas, basketball goals, or any other fixture or signs, notices, or visual displays of any kind to the dwelling exterior without the landlord's written permission.

Cable or satellite TV. No cable line or satellite TV can be added, attached, or installed by the residents or agents of residents without the written approval of landlord or management.

Illegal drugs. No illegal drugs are permitted on premises—stored, used, or sold.

5. Maintenance, Repairs, and Emergencies

Major repair requests. Residents agree to make all requests for repair, beyond normal property upkeep, to the landlord in writing in order that the landlord may schedule and arrange for repair in an orderly manner and ensure that repairs that are most vital are done first. The landlord is not responsible for repairs that have not been requested in writing from resident to landlord. Residents may contact the owner or manager by e-mail at the following address: _____, or use request forms mailed to the following address: _____.

Maintenance inspection. There will be a property inspection approximately every six months. A property inspection report will be written indicating all (if any) damage to the property by residents, who will be responsible for paying for damages within 30 calendar days.

Upkeep/property maintenance. If residents fail to make minor repairs as part of the normal upkeep of the residence, the landlord may pay for needed repairs to be completed and the repair expense will be due and required from the residents.

Emergency contacts. Residents will only use/contact names from a list of personnel or companies provided by the landlord to call in the event of emergency response needed.

Entry. Residents understand that the landlord has the right to enter the dwelling at any and all reasonable times (with proper advance notice given) for repair work, to inspect for compliance with this agreement, or show prospective residents. Therefore, no locks will be added to the doors without first getting permission and giving a duplicate key to the landlord.

Liens upon property. Residents have no authority to incur any debt or make any charge against the landlord or assign or create any lien upon said leased property for any work, utilities, or materials furnished to the same.

6. Pets and Vehicles

No pets. No pets or animals of *any* kind are permitted on the premises. This restriction includes, and is not limited to, dogs, cats, birds, fish, reptiles, rodents, ferrets, etc.

Pet deposit/fees. If a pet is permitted, pet-owning residents agree to pay an additional security deposit of $_____, which is refundable and returned at the end of the rental term if not needed to cover damages or restoration of the rental. There is also a $_____ fee to have the unit sprayed after they move out. Residents further agree to pay a pet fee of $_____ per month for each pet kept on the premises.

Authorized pets. The following pet is the only authorized pet permitted and is described as follows: _____. A picture is attached to the rental agreement. Acceptance of this pet does not authorize acceptance of any other pet, and any other animal discovered on the premises would be a violation of this rental agreement. All authorized pets must have their shots up to date, and residents must be able to show the paperwork to prove it on request. The resident is also required to obtain insurance that would cover possible damages and injuries that may be caused by pets.

Dog/cat owners. Dogs will be leashed at all times and at no time will dogs be allowed to roam freely. Additional conditions for dog owners include the following:

_____.

For cat owners, the following conditions apply:

_____.

Strays. Any animal not on the application or listed in the rental agreement and discovered on the premises will be considered a stray. All strays will be reported to the proper authority and removed at residents' expense. Any residents found providing shelter at said property to a stray are subject to a fine of not less than $100 plus the cost of removing the stray and repairing any damage the landlord has deemed the stray has caused.

Vehicle(s). Vehicle(s) must be registered with the landlord and are limited to the number stated on the original application unless written permission is granted otherwise. Absolutely no car repair is permitted on the premises. Any nonregistered, abandoned, or inoperative vehicle on the property for more than seven days will be removed at car owner's expense. Licensed vehicles may be parked only in garages, driveways, designated parking spaces (if provided), or on the street. The residents agree to only park vehicles on premises as listed here, automobiles(s) license number(s): _____. All other cars remaining more than three days will be towed away at car owner's expense.

Recreational vehicles. Residents agree never to park or store a motor home, camper trailer, or any recreational vehicle on the premises.

7. Alterations, Upkeep, and Improvements

Alterations. Residents agree and understand that they are not permitted to paint or alter the dwelling in any way without first getting written permission. This includes changing or installing locks, or attaching nails or screws to walls.

Furnace filters. Residents agree, at their own expense, to change the furnace filters at least once every three months.

Yard upkeep. Residents agree to keep lawn and shrubbery in a clipped and trimmed condition, and care for and remove weeds from flowerbeds and planting areas.

Snow/ice. Residents agree to keep sidewalks and driveways clear from snow/ice. Snow/ice will not be left unattended for more than twenty-four (24) hours. Should the landlord have to hire someone to rectify the situation, residents agree to pay a minimum charge of $_____.

Garbage/litter removal. Residents will put their garbage in a garbage receptacle with a lid. If one is provided by management at the beginning of the rental term, the resident is responsible for keeping and using it as well as a replacement if the original becomes damaged or disappears. Management will hire someone to pick up any litter, trash, spilled garbage, and general debris after being neglected for more than one week at residents' expense.

Smoking. Smoking is permitted/not permitted. At the time of move-out, residents who smoke automatically assume the responsibility to have walls and ceilings repainted, carpets professionally cleaned, and other smoke-damaged areas, such as blinds, cleaned.

Batteries in smoke detectors. Residents acknowledge that the premises were equipped with a smoke detector that was operating at time of move-in. Residents agree to periodically (twice yearly before scheduled home inspections) test the smoke detector, replace the batteries as needed, and inform the owner or manager immediately of any malfunction. A $_____ fee will be charged if any inspection necessitates battery replacement.

Pest control. Residents acknowledge that the rental is free of pests at the time of occupancy. Residents are responsible for keeping the premises free of pests and paying for pest control service, if such services are desired and/or needed.

8. Damages, Liabilities, and Insurance

Property negligence. Residents agree to pay for any damage caused by negligence on their part or the part of their children or pets. Residents further agree to pay for the repair of any broken windows or drain stoppages, regardless of fault, while residing at this dwelling. Residents will not allow such conditions to go unreported for more than 48 hours. Residents further agree not to leave windows in an open position during any inclement weather and to be held responsible for damages from noncompliance with this clause.

Liquid-filled furniture. Residents agree not to have any liquid-filled furniture in the premises without permission of the landlord. If permission is granted, residents agree to have the waterbed or any other liquid-filled furniture installed under particular guidelines provided by the owner and obtain insurance to cover possible losses that may be caused by such items.

Notice of absence. Residents will give the landlord notice of an anticipated extended absence from the property in excess of three days. Notification to the landlord will be made not later than the first day of extended absence. During any such absence of residents, the landlord may enter the property at times deemed reasonably necessary to protect the property and any possessions of the landlord on or in the property. For failure to notify the landlord of extended absence that results in damage to the property, residents will be held responsible.

Removal of landlord's property. Residents will be held liable for landlord's possessions removed without permission and subject to civil and/or criminal charges.

Utility reconnecting. If there is an occurrence whereby utilities are discontinued at the rental premises for more than three days, the landlord, at residents' expense, may choose to reinstate utilities in landlord's name and the cost of such process and the amount of such utilities will be charged to residents as added rent.

Notification of problems. Residents agree to report any roof leaks or plumbing, electrical, heating, or air-conditioning problem or to immediately report any property defect that the landlord is responsible for and which could cause possible injury to residents or further damage to the property. Failure to notify the owner or manager makes residents liable for damage to the property resulting from slow or non-notification of the problem.

Swimming pools/trampolines/playground equipment. No swimming pools of any kind, trampolines, playground equipment, or any other attractive nuisances are permitted on the premises without the owner's written permission. If such items are permitted, additional insurance or other requirements may be needed by residents.

Equipment overload. Residents will not install, use, or permit to be installed or used, any equipment of any kind that will require alteration of, or create an overload on, any gas, water, heating, electrical, sewerage, drainage, or air-conditioning systems of the said property without prior written consent of the landlord.

Renter's insurance. Residents acknowledge that owner's insurance does not cover personal property damage caused by fire, theft, burglary, breakage, electrical connections, rain, war, acts of God, acts of others, and/or any other causes, nor shall owner be held liable for such losses. Residents are hereby advised/required to obtain their own insurance policy to cover any personal losses.

Mildew. The landlord and residents have inspected the premises prior to lease and noticed no sign of moisture or mildew contamination. Residents shall remove any visible moisture accumulation in or on the premises, including walls, floors, ceilings, and bathroom fixtures. Residents further agree to mop up spills and thoroughly dry areas with moisture as soon as possible after occurrence and regularly allow air to circulate (e.g., using bathroom fans while showering or bathing) and keep climate and moisture in the premises at reasonable levels. Residents shall promptly notify landlord in writing of any excessive moisture, plumbing leaks, drips, sweating pipes, or standing water inside the premises (that resident was unable to remove) or in any common area. Residents also agree to notify landlord promptly of malfunctioning fans and any water overflow from the bathroom, kitchen, or laundry facilities where the water may have permeated the cabinets or walls. Residents shall be held liable for damages sustained to the premises or to occupants as a result of residents' failure to comply with these terms.

Explosives, inflammables, or hazardous conditions. Residents will not use any method for heating (other than normal methods provided) without special agreement. Residents are not permitted to keep any kerosene, burning fluid, combustible materials, or explosives of any kind in the dwelling. Further, no hazardous conditions may be created that might cause fire or increase insurance rates for the premises.

9. Renewals and Move-Outs

Deposit returned. The security deposit will not be allowed to cover last month's rent or any future rent payment. Deposits will only be returned _____ days after the resident vacates, the unit is inspected, and if the following conditions are met:

- Full terms of rental agreement are completed.
- No damage is done to the premises.
- All unpaid charges, fees, and rents have been paid.
- In addition, _____.

Deposits will be mailed to your new forwarding address.

Moving notice. Residents agree to give _____ day(s) written notice before they intend to move to qualify for receiving any of the security deposit back.

End-of-term assistance. At the end of agreement, residents agree to assist the owner by permitting the owner or manager to show property to prospective residents prior to moving. If a new qualified applicant agrees to rent the property once vacant before the last day of occupancy of vacating residents, vacating residents are eligible to receive a $_____ bonus on top of whatever deposit to which they will be entitled.

Military clause. If residents are in or hereafter become members of the United States Armed Forces, U.S. State Department, U.S. AID, or any federal government agency on extended active duty and are transferred under PCS orders during the lease term, they may terminate this lease by giving landlord thirty (30) days written notice to that effect, together with a certified copy of their orders. Such notice will cancel this lease on the last day of the following month. A transfer out of the area is defined as at least fifty (50) miles from the rented premises.

10. Correspondence, Acceptance, and Agreement

Assigned manager. _____ is the person designated by the management company to manage the premises and to receive and give receipt for all notices and demands upon the management company at our business address: _____.

Office hours. Residents will call manager's office between _____ and _____ weekdays for business-related matters. For emergencies, outside of business hours, call _____.

No oral agreements/amendments. The agreements contained in the lease set forth the entire understanding of the parties as regards the lease provisions of this agreement and will not be changed or terminated orally. This agreement may only be amended, modified, or added to by written instrument only.

Condition acceptance. Residents acknowledge that they have examined the premises and that said premises, all furnishings, fixtures, plumbing, heating, electrical facilities, all items listed on the attached property condition checklist, if any, and/or all other items provided by the owner are all clean and in satisfactory condition except as may be indicated elsewhere in this agreement. Residents agree to keep premises and all items in good order and good condition, and immediately pay for costs to repair and/or replace any portion of the above damaged by residents and/or guests. At the termination of this agreement, all of above items in this provision shall be returned to owner in clean and satisfactory condition except for reasonable wear and tear, and the premises shall be free of all personal property and trash not belonging to owner. It is agreed that all dirt, holes, tears, burns, and stains of any size or amount in the carpets, drapes, walls, fixtures, and/or any other part of the premises do not constitute reasonable wear and tear.

Nice landlord caution. Residents will not mistake landlord's "niceness" as "weakness."

Enforcement. Owner's acceptance of rent or failure to enforce any term in this lease is not a waiver of any owner's right. Should any provision of this agreement conflict with new laws and be found to be invalid or unenforceable, those provisions are severable. The remainder of this agreement will not be affected thereby and each term and provision herein will be valid and remain in force to the fullest extent permitted by law.

Truthfulness of rental application. Information on the rental application submitted by residents has been the reason for landlord to rent the premises to residents. If any material facts in the rental application are found untrue or if the premises are occupied by anyone other than the residents as stated in the application, the landlord will have the right to terminate this lease.

Joint liability. Each person signing this agreement as a resident is jointly and severally (*together* and *separately*) responsible for all the terms of this agreement including the *full* rent amount and for any damages that become due.

VI. WARNING ABOUT ILLEGAL CLAUSES

Just because a landlord may include a clause in the rental agreement—and even if the resident signs the agreement—that doesn't mean the clause is enforceable. Many landlords, perhaps unknowingly, have illegal clauses in their agreements. The problem is that a judge may throw out the entire agreement if an illegal clause is discovered.

The following types of clauses are somewhat common; however, avoid using them because they aren't legal in most states:

- Clauses that say residents give up any of their legal rights, especially ones found in the state's landlord-tenant laws
- Clauses that limit landlord liability where the landlord is normally responsible
- Clauses that allow a landlord to enter the rental for any reason without first giving proper notice
- Clauses that require residents to pay all damages even if they're due to landlord's negligence
- Clauses that allow landlords to immediately seize residents' property or evict residents (without going through legal eviction proceedings) if they fall behind in rent

VII. MONTH-TO-MONTH AGREEMENT VERSUS FIXED-TERM LEASE

I often get asked: "Which is better, a month-to-month rental agreement or a fixed-term, one-year lease?" I favor the month-to-month agreement for several reasons. In a month-to-month agreement, the landlord has the option of raising the rent during the year (with proper short-term notice; i.e., 30 days in most states) if he/she deems it necessary to cover extreme hikes in utility prices, unexpected price surges, or major expenses affecting the operation of the rental. Along with having the ability to change the rental rate, landlords with a month-to-month agreement can make other modifications to the rental agreement. In most states, a reason doesn't have to be given. If you have a fixed-term lease, you can't raise the rent or make major changes to the terms during the lease term.

The landlord with a month-to-month agreement can evict a resident relatively quickly in most states for problems other than nonpayment of rent. The landlord with a fixed-length lease has far greater difficulty evicting a resident for areas not as cut-and-dried as nonpayment of rent.

In theory, you should be able to evict residents for violating the lease, assuming that the lease states such a violation is grounds for eviction. However, most courts won't force residents to honor the lease like it does with a landlord. It's extremely difficult to evict residents for lease violations other than nonpayments. Many judges give residents several chances to correct the rental violation; some judges may not enforce a clause they consider unreasonable or petty.

When residents leave before a fixed-length lease is up, in theory, they owe rent through the rest of the lease term or until the place is re-rented, whichever comes first. They also owe all costs of re-renting the property. For you to collect anything, however, you must "mitigate" damage, which means try to re-rent the unit as soon as possible. Obviously, it's to your advantage to rent it quickly, not letting it sit empty as a target for vandalism or cold weather. Once you acquire new residents, your former residents are let off the hook for the balance of the agreement because it's illegal to collect double rent. Unless your place sits empty for a long time, you'll probably not get a judgment for more than you'd get from residents who skip out from under a month-to-month rental agreement.

Even if you were fortunate enough to get a large judgment covering more than one month of rent owed, you still have the bigger challenge of collecting the money due from residents who skipped out. (See Step 7 for collection tactics.) In my opinion, the month-to-month agreement has more advantages than the fixed-length lease. Besides, you can create customer loyalty programs that encourage residents to stay three years and longer, no matter the legal length of the agreement. If you only use a fixed-term lease to get people to stay 12 months, I dare say you're merely "hoping" again. (The retention ideas in Step 9 offer effective alternative strategies.)

7

GET YOUR MONEY

"Never chase the money. Just start eviction."
—JAY DECIMA

In your new resident orientation, having a people-centered attitude doesn't mean you don't take time to stress the absolute necessity for rent payments to be made on time and any penalties
for not doing so. Collecting rents from residents is one area in which
tension often develops between the landlord and the resident. However,
I've discovered that some payment methods work out better for both
parties. By setting up automatic payment plans, discussed in this step,
you don't have to allow collecting money to become an issue between
you and your residents. There is more than one way to set up such plans,
which I call worry-free payment methods. Follow these steps to increase
the odds that you'll get all monies residents owe you—whether they
choose one of the automatic payment methods or pay using "old-fashioned" methods.

I'll also discuss what to do when the inevitable occurs and a resident
is late, a check bounces, or a resident misses a payment altogether. I always prepare in advance the action steps I'll take once a challenge occurs. I'll even reveal what to do when residents still owing money move
out and how you can recover the debt.

I. DROP THE AMATEUR LANDLORD APPROACH

A resident was upset with her new landlord for charging her extra because she was more than ten days late with her rent. She said she'd always paid her rent late, but she'd always paid it. When she learned that her new landlord expected rent on time, she wondered what could be done about this evil, greedy owner.

This attitude, which is surprisingly common among residents—even good ones—is fostered by amateur landlords who are permissive, not realizing that their leniency causes difficulties to a greater extent later. Their amateur approach paves the way for lack of success in collecting rents on time. Many landlords don't even realize that, for most states, you're not legally required to allow a grace period after rent is due. If that's the case, always enforce your on-time policy on the date due (no grace period) and, if not paid, start eviction proceedings immediately.

When residents find that you permit late payments for rent, they won't place the proper importance on making on-time payments. In fact, they'll lose respect for your management. Your costliest result from having an "easy" payment policy is the complete loss of rents due to eviction and skips. Landlords who allow residents to be a few weeks late soon find them a month behind in rent. At that point, they owe two month's rent and the amount due seems astronomical. Some may think it's easier to move than to pay the back rent. Worse yet, they may test how long they can stay without paying anything. What policies can you implement to avoid that?

I. Let Residents Know They Will Be Held Accountable

Tell your residents from the beginning that they'll be held accountable for paying on time. Remind them at the beginning of each year; don't just lay down the ground rules on paper (in your rental agreement). Let them know that you'll report information concerning any nonpayments to all three major credit bureaus, so that potential employers, banks, home mortgage companies, and any other creditors they may want to do business with in the future can access the information. Tell them up front that the reputation they establish with you will last many years. This can have positive benefits, though, because you're helping them build their credibility—and credit.

2. Enforce Your Rules and On-Time Payments

The biggest collection time waster average landlords use is sending a reminder letter or a late notice after the due date. It notifies a resident that payment is already late. Some even send a series of reminders that get harsher in tone. Stop doing that! The first, most effective, and only notice that you should send is a "pay or quit" notice. Depending on the state where you live, it may be for a three-day, five-day, seven-day, or ten-day period. This notice officially starts the legal eviction process.

Rent has to be paid on time; that's fundamental to operating your rental properties. If residents don't develop the habit of paying on time during the first three months, your headaches will begin. Once formed, a habit tends to be self-perpetuating and difficult to change. That's why it's crucial that you clearly establish, educate, and enforce an on-time payment policy during the first three months. Don't show any leniency or make exceptions for unpaid rent. Start eviction procedures immediately, if necessary, and specify additional charges for rent, service, or court fees in your lease. By aggressively enforcing the necessity for on-time rent payments in the first quarter, you help residents develop good habits and maintain a steady cash flow to yourself. It's no time to be Mr. Nice Guy.

II. REQUEST AUTOMATIC PAYMENTS

If you're just starting in this business, I suggest informing residents that one of your three standard worry-free methods of collecting rent is by direct rent deposits (the second being automatic payroll deduction and a third being debit card collection). Don't encourage them to pay the old-fashioned way by mailing checks or, worse yet, dropping off cash. Rents are the lifeblood of the rental property business; take control.

Announce to new residents and old that they never have to worry about late fees again—they have the option of paying rent automatically each month. When they apply to rent your property, simply ask which checking account they'll be using during the term of the rental, then request permission to draft or debit that account on an agreed-upon date each month. It's one of your standard worry-free methods of rent collection. Another version of this option is electronic funds transfer (EFT).

Explain that automatic rent payment comes with advantages. Residents will actually like the convenience because they won't have to scramble to mail checks on time to avoid late fees. In addition, they may qualify for monthly money vouchers credited to a homebuyers program for timely payments throughout the year. (See Step 10 for more on that idea.)

Some landlords require residents whose rents are paid by third parties to use an autopay plan. For example, parents of college-age students like the convenience because they don't have to physically put money in a student's bank account each month. Would you believe some college students have been known to receive housing money from Mom and Dad, then use it to party all weekend? An automatic payment plan direct from the parent's account to the landlord's removes the temptation from students not to pay the rent.

The two most common forms of automatic rent payment plans are electronic/automatic paper drafts or EFTs.

1. How Automatic Paper Drafts Work

During the new resident orientation, get written permission from residents to use preauthorized checks for paying rent. With this method, there's no computer access into their checking accounts (therefore nothing for them to be fearful about). Their payments get re-created each month by either the landlord or a third-party company providing this service. You receive and deposit the checks each month on an agreed-upon date. Because you control the checks, there's no chance for the bank to make mistakes on your residents' accounts. Using this system, you can even hold a check for a "good" resident when an infrequent emergency occurs. This form of automatic payment has been successfully used by health clubs and insurance companies since the 1970s.

2. Use Electronic Fund Transfer (EFT) or Direct Rent Deposits

Once again, frustrations and uncertainties dealing with mailed checks don't need to exist. Consider getting set up to receive EFTs or direct rent deposits, which are automatic electronic rent payments. Each month, the appropriate rent amount transfers from your residents' checking accounts to your checking account—an electronic process that eliminates checks. Direct rent deposits occur through the Automated Clearing House (ACH) payment network—the same payment network banks use to transmit payroll for millions of employees through direct deposit (thus the coined term *direct rent deposit*).

Direct rent deposits usually require residents to complete a one-time setup, which gives you their checking account information (generally by submitting a voided check). Direct rent deposits are safe for residents because Federal Regulation E (Electronic Funds Transfer Act of 1978) safeguards consumers against the inappropriate movement of funds from their account.

Remember, you have no guarantee that residents have sufficient funds in their accounts to cover rent. However, with direct rent deposits, you learn about insufficient funds quickly—far sooner than with paper checks.

When you use direct rent deposits, you eliminate paper checks and deposit slips as well as the possibility of mail delays, check fraud, misplaced checks, and more. All transfers happen electronically so there are no checks to write or misplace, no mail delays, and no trips to the banks needed. Everyone saves time!

3. Get Residents' Authorization to Charge Rent to Their Debit or Credit Cards

You can use residents' debit or credit cards to your advantage. When residents sign the lease, have them authorize you in writing to automat-

---

F *ind* **C** *ompanies at* **M** *r L a n d l o r d . c o m*

I often get calls from excited landlords who've heard me at a seminar encouraging automatic payment plans. They've run into a stumbling block implementing the system and complain, "Jeffrey, my bank can't set me up for automatic drafts or electronic funds transfers because I'm not a merchant and I don't have a storefront." Or they want to charge hundreds of dollars. Or the user needs a computer and training.

The solution? Search for national third-party companies that specialize in working with landlords by helping them receive automatic payment plans, including automatic paper drafts or direct rent deposits. Go to MrLandlord.com for a list of national third-party companies that have agreed to work with my subscribers.

ically charge their debit or credit cards each month. This is becoming a viable collection method for landlords of all sizes—though one possible drawback is that residents can "dispute" a payment and have the credit card company reverse the charges.

A Convenience for Residents and Landlords

Credit card issuers like Visa want to boost profits by encouraging consumers to use cards for recurring transactions such as utility bills, car payments, and rent. Nearly one of two consumers uses credit cards to make at least one recurring monthly payment—typically for health club memberships, Internet services, or newspaper subscription. Convenience was the main reason, though 45 percent of the users said they benefited from lower stress knowing bills are paid on time, and 17 percent said they enjoyed a financial reward such as frequent-flier miles or discounts.

One property manager of a national company began accepting Visa payments at some of its properties a few years ago. Since then, over 350,000 units in 46 states accept Visa payments. Visa says a recent poll showed that 40 percent of those who are aware of the option use it. Other management surveys indicate that 20 to 40 percent of residents offered the option to pay by credit or debit cards do so. Consumers also have the option of using debit cards to pay recurring bills. With a debit card, the bill is deducted directly from a checking account.

By paying rent in this way, residents seem to be less price sensitive. "Offering residents the automatic bill payment option helps avoid that moment of truth each month," according to a Visa press release. "When residents write a check they inevitably ask themselves, 'Am I paying too much for what I'm getting? Should I look around to see if I can get a better deal elsewhere?'"

Residents have commented that the ability to charge rent, security deposits, and other fees was one of the reasons they chose to live in a particular community. Also, 80 percent of landlords and managers reported that accepting credit and debit card payments made renting apartments easier, and 83 percent reported that the service increased the number of payments received on time.

4. Automatic Payroll Deduction

Another way to collect rents automatically is getting residents' permission to have rent deducted from their paychecks. This works well if their employers are already set up to handle automatic payroll deductions from their employees' paychecks. For example, in my area, residents who are in the military and working for certain parts of the government can easily have payroll deductions arranged. You provide the checking account information where the funds should be deposited and a resident fills out the appropriate forms.

Please note, however, that the amount of payroll deduction is probably in equal amounts for each pay period. If your residents get paid every two weeks, then the deduction and payment to you will occur every two weeks, which is fine if they chose the payday rent payment plan (discussed in depth in Step 8). A variation of the payday plan will need to be used if the resident's pay period occurs twice a month (e.g., on the 1st and 15th), which is different than every two weeks. Both ways can work, however, it's important that both you and the resident clearly understand when and how much rent will be deducted and paid each pay period. Spell it out clearly in your rental agreement.

III. OFFER INCENTIVES FOR TRADITIONAL PAYMENT METHODS

If you're still collecting rent the old-fashioned way by accepting rent checks, consider these ideas.

1. Use the Discounted Rent Approach

A common incentive landlords offer for getting checks on time is a discounted rent policy that allows residents to pay less (anywhere from $20 to $100 less) than the normal or gross rent. They receive this discount by meeting certain obligations—most basically, ensuring payment is received at a designated place by the 1st of the month (or even a few days before).

Landlords start to define discounted rent by deciding how much net rent they want for their rental based on how much the market will bear. Then they advertise this net rental amount. When prospects apply, they're told that the advertised price is the discounted rental price, which is what residents are required to pay as long as payments are received by an agreed-upon date. If rents are paid after that date, landlords request an inflated amount ($20 to $100 greater), which is called the "normal" or "gross" rent due. They list this amount in the lease. Doing this eliminates the need for imposing a late charge.

Though the rental income for timely payments may be identical using the two approaches—discount or net rent and gross rent versus normal net rent and late charges—psychologically and economically, the former approach has distinct advantages. The discount approach makes for better landlord-resident relations because it rewards people for timely payments rather than penalizing them for late payments.

This distinction may come into play when taking a delinquent resident to court or when selling your rental property. In many states, judges

---

Learn from a Landlord's Experience

"I just started using the discount rent clause I learned from one of your seminars. I had a new resident who would pay me a discounted rent religiously on the first of the month of $550. Normal rent, if not paid by the first, is $625. This went on for five months. Then I finally got that phone call, 'Well, uh, it'll be a few days before I can get the money from the credit union.' The resident came back four days later with a check for $625 like the contract specified. No questions asked. Thanks for the idea! It worked for me."

Please note the difference of amount due in the above letter when rent is paid after the first—$75. Because this difference is larger than the usual $20 to $25, you often get greater cooperation from your residents. This larger-than-normal amount is possible when used with a discounted rent clause. Most judges won't enforce your late charges, as part of the rent due, that are a large percentage of the rent (anything above 5 percent is often considered an unreasonable late charge). Some judges won't grant or allow landlords to include any late charges as part of a judgment. Under the discount rent plan, you may have less of a problem enforcing payment due of the gross amount listed in the agreement or getting a judgment for the normal gross lease amount, if it comes to that.

don't reward late charges or consider them excessive. But under a discounted rent policy, you can get judgment for the gross rental amount stated in your agreement without having to prove actual damages; no matter how much of the discount was loss by the resident.

Also, when appraisals are done on income-producing properties, part of the appraisal is based on the gross rental income, not including late charges. That way, two properties receiving the same amount of income each month may show a difference of thousands of dollars in market value.

In a few states, however, landlord-tenant laws don't permit rental discounts. Check state and local laws. Also check whether late fees can legally be enforced, if there are legal limits on the amount or percentage that can be charged, and on what date late charges can begin. Your state may require a certain time period before late charges can commence.

2. Offer Prepayment Credit to Cover Utilities

Another possible incentive is to include a clause in your rental agreement that not only encourages on-time rent payment, but helps to ensure that the water bill is paid. Here's a sample clause:

> RENT: The normal rent for the premises is $_____ payable and due on the first of each month. PREPAYMENT CREDIT: Any rent received prior to the 20th of the month will qualify for a prepayment credit of $_____. The credit will be rebated quarterly by the management to the resident in the form of a check made payable to a utility company to which the resident is responsible according to the terms of this agreement. (Utility of landlord's preference is the water authority.)

3. Use Monthly Drawings as Incentives

Some landlords use prizes as an incentive for encouraging that rent checks are sent and received in a timely manner. For example, if the rent is paid on time, the resident's name is put in a "hat." On a designated day of the month, a name is drawn and a prize given. Prizes include mixers, coffee makers (the new fancy versions), DVD players, and items costing the landlord up to $50. The landlord also circulates a newsletter for residents who enjoy seeing their names in print. Other landlords actually offer a cash drawing of $50 or more to the one prizewinner drawn each month. Again, the use of a monthly newsletter that announces the drawing winner can serve as a reminder to mail next month's rent. You will need a few residents (four or more) before considering this idea. Even if a resident "wins" three or four times a year, offering only one prize per month will cost less than giving several residents a discount or rebate each month.

IV. REMIND RESIDENTS OF THEIR OBLIGATIONS

1. Formal Approach: Send a Two-Part Invoice

If you normally receive rent payments by mail, send a two-part slip or invoice to residents five to seven days *before* rent is due—both as a reminder and a record of rent due. Include a self-addressed envelope for residents to drop their payments in the mailbox. Using a two-part slip, residents keep one part that itemizes when rent is due, how much is due, the late fee (if any), and the date when a late fee is due. They send the second part, your copy, with payment. This increases the chances that residents send their payments correctly and on time.

2. Informal Approach: Use Reminder Envelopes and Rent Reminders

Send residents a self-addressed stamped envelope (SASE), making sure they receive these envelopes in time to mail their rent checks before rent is due.

Send an informal note (see sample in sidebar) to all residents seven days before rent is due. This reminds them to pay rent and indicates how to save money by avoiding late fees.

3. Give Out Key Tags with the Payment Address

When residents move in, give them their keys on key tags with the name and address to where rent is mailed. The key tag will serve as a rent

H *i* **T** *here!*

"SAVE MONEY"
YOU CAN AVOID LATE FEES.

Rent payments are coming due. If you choose to, mail your rental amount to us at _____, and please allow at least five days for delivery. It doesn't count if I do not get it on time. Do not trust the postal system to get it to us fast. Remember, if payment is received after the due date, regardless of when it was mailed, there will be additional payment required.

Sincerely,

reminder, plus tell residents where to mail the rent in case they forget the address. On the key tags, also include the lines: Drop in any mailbox. Return postage guaranteed. This increases the chance that lost keys are returned.

V. PROVIDE ALTERNATIVE WAYS FOR PAYING

1. Have Rents Paid Directly to Bank

If you have residents who like to pay in cash, set up a rent collection system with a local bank that has branches near where you own rentals. Residents make rent deposits directly into your checking account at the bank; they have no other access to this account except to make deposits. Open an account used solely for deposits for a specified rental address, with access—and without added cost—to be able to check and withdraw from the account through the month (perhaps done automatically). The end of the month statement will be your rent income record.

For tracking several properties tied to the same bank account, give your properties a code number or resident identification to be used when paying the rent. For example, rent for #03 is $403 so the resident deposits $403. Rent for property #08 is $408 so the resident deposits $408, and so on. This will help you determine which residents have paid when you're verifying payments by phone or online. Alternatively, you could have a different bank account for each property.

What does this system do? For the resident, it lets them pay in cash (no money order or stamp costs) at convenient bank branch locations. For the landlord, you aren't at risk collecting cash and having residents come to your home. You've eliminated a lot of time-consuming rent collection. You have less paperwork because the bank "writes" the rent receipts (deposit slips) and "creates" a rent record (monthly deposit record). And checks don't get hung up in the postal service. This system even encourages residents to pay on time because they feel more obligated to pay on time when paying a bank. Note: Tell residents to keep deposit receipts for their records as proof of payment in case there's ever a question.

2. Become a Protective Payee for AFDC Clients

Collecting rent owed by public assistance recipients, such as those receiving Aid to Families with Dependent Children (AFDC) grants, can be troubling. In your state, ask the AFDC payee to make you the "protective payee" for the AFDC grant, and you can cash the government check that comes in the mail in your name. After cashing the check, apply the correct amount to the rent and give the balance to AFDC payee. AFDC clients voluntarily designate protective payees, but you need to establish a clear paper trail to show that you didn't retain funds improperly or hold any amount not due to you for rent.

This method of rent payment is especially helpful in preventing another person (usually a close relative) from taking funds away from the resident payee before rent is paid. (Someone other than your primary resident can be the root of the problem.) Explain to the AFDC payee that using this method would keep them from being evicted and going into a homeless situation. (The state government has a standard form for protective payee status that you'd request, fill out, and return.)

VI. TAKE ACTION WHEN RESIDENTS MISS A PAYMENT

Do not delay in taking action if payment is not made on the due date.

1. Start by Having Correct Documentation of What Is Due

Always keep accurate records of all payments made by your residents, so there is never a question about how much is owed. You'd be surprised to know how many landlords actually lose track of what is owed by their residents.

Keep receipts for past-due rents in chronological order. Never write a receipt for a current rental period if the resident is in arrears for an earlier period. All rent monies paid should apply to the earlier period first. Here's why.

Suppose a resident is one month behind in his rent and you sue him for nonpayment. Suppose also that on January 1 he pays December's rent, but you give him a receipt covering the month of January. In court, the resident produces your receipt for the current month of January and tells the judge he lost the December receipt. The judge has to assume that your resident is telling the truth because you can't prove conclusively that he didn't pay for December. The fact that you do not have a copy of his December rent payment doesn't prove anything. It's only what you have that counts. How can you prove that the December rent receipt never existed? Stating under oath that he didn't pay for December doesn't prove anything either. It's your word against your resident's. The judge has to base his decision on the existence of the resident's January rent receipt. The receipt suddenly becomes important because it does prove that the resident paid for January, and if he paid for January, then he probably did pay for December. He wins.

You lose one month's rent. Losing one month's rent can be very important, can't it? So I repeat—never write a rent receipt for a current period if the resident is in arrears for an earlier period.

2. Begin Legal Eviction Proceeding with a Notice to the Resident

This means serving a resident with a notice to pay or quit as soon as rent is past due and permitted by law. If the resident does not pay within the specified time, immediately file an unlawful detainer. Refer to your state eviction laws and your attorney.

3. Contact the Lease Cosigner, If There Is One

An owner always takes a certain amount of risk when he leases his property. The prospective resident may not pay the rent or may damage the premises. Even if a court rules in the landlord's favor, the judgment may be difficult to collect. Some of the risk can be reduced by requiring a cosigner to personally guarantee the lease contract.

The guarantor or cosigner, who is typically more creditworthy than the resident, agrees to be liable on the lease. He promises that if the resident doesn't pay, he, the guarantor will. The first thing to remember is that the guaranty should be executed at the same time as the original rental agreement with the resident, not later.

Upon execution of the guaranty, the guarantor becomes liable for rental damages, costs, and attorney fees to the same extent that the resident is responsible for them under the terms of the rental agreement. Care should be taken in drafting the guaranty to make sure that the guarantor is responsible for all obligations of the lease to the full extent that the resident is.

Assuming that the lease includes a valid guaranty and the resident defaults, how should the guarantor be dealt with? Unless the lease expressly provides that the guarantor's liability is contingent upon receiving notice of the default, the guarantor does not have the right to be notified of a default.

Nonetheless, we strongly recommend that the guarantor be given all notices of default. The guarantor's name should be included, for example, on notice to pay rent or quit, and he, too, should be served with the notice. Serving the notice on the guarantor may avoid a lawsuit and give the guarantor an opportunity to cure the default.

4. Use Promissory Notes

When residents fall behind in rent, ask for a signed promissory note if they want you to "work" with them. Have the note state admission that: (a) the resident owes you money, and (b) the resident didn't withhold rent because of needed repairs or code violations.

By admitting they owe you in writing, residents cannot say later that the nonpayment was to offset some horrible thing you did to them. It also protects you if they try to say both parties had a special deal in which they didn't have to pay rent for a certain period of time in exchange for maintenance work, or for some other false reason.

Showing the judge the promissory note when a resident starts making up lies will cut the conversation right off. The judge will say, "Did you sign this?" If the answer is yes, the judge will say, "Guilty. Pay up. Judgment for the landlord. Next case." It should also be noted that promissory notes are assumable.

VII. DEALING WITH PROBLEM PAYMENTS: LATE PAYMENTS, BOUNCED CHECKS, UNSIGNED CHECKS, AND STOLEN CHECKS

Prepare for the worst even if your residents aren't prepared. Sometimes your otherwise "good" residents may face circumstances over which they seem to have no control. Because you know that it's only a matter of time before some of your good residents will have financial problems, prepare ahead of time to show them how to handle their problems. Contact all possible agencies, organizations, or churches in your area that provide short-term financial assistance for housing.

Make a list of such agencies and churches in your area so that your residents can make the effort to call those listed on your financial emergency housing assistance list if they are experiencing temporary financial difficulties. Using your list, the residents should be able to generate enough money, before eviction takes place, to cover one or two months' rent during a tough time.

1. Use the Suspended Charges Approach

One variation of the "hardnosed landlording" techniques that one landlord has found successful is this: The lease includes a $25 late fee if the rent is not received or deposited by the first of the month.

There's an additional daily fee for each day past the first that the rent remains unpaid. When otherwise excellent residents miss a payment, which is generally due to oversight or being out of town, he itemizes the late fee so they realize the impact of late payments. Then he tells them that he will "suspend" the late fee *this time only* as long as all future payments are on time. Any future late payment will cause the suspended amount to become due, as well as any other new late fees.

This avoids unnecessarily penalizing the residents he doesn't want to lose, but still keeps his landlord policies consistent. It also usually gets residents to pay the future month's rent several days early!

2. Not Enough in Resident's Account? Not a Problem

Whether you realize it or not, you can still collect money from a bounced check if you follow the strategy used by a landlord I know.

When this landlord has a strong feeling he won't collect his rent money after receiving a bad check for $500, he goes to the resident's bank and gets a deposit slip. Before going to the bank he calls the bank, gives the resident's bank account number, and asks if a check in the amount written would clear. If the answer is no, he calls back at another time and asks if a check with a lower amount would clear. He repeats this process until he determines how much is needed to make the check for $500 good. If $60 is the magic number, he writes in the resident's account number on the blank deposit slip and deposits $60 cash. Then he takes out the $500 bad check the resident had given him and cashes it because there's now enough in the account. Having $440 is a lot better than nothing at all.

3. What to Do When the Check Isn't Signed

Have you ever gotten a check from a resident that wasn't signed, either in error or as a ruse to delay payment? Have you received a check that was wrongly marked "payment in full"? Have you wondered what you could do with them and not lose the money you were owed? Well, here are some solutions that you will be happy to hear.

The procedure for guaranteeing an unsigned check is simple and straightforward. Write "over" on the signature line. Turn the check over and write or type "lack of signature guaranteed" followed by your signature, typed name, title, company name, and account number. Deposit the check as usual. You can also cash a check marked "payment in full." Federal law permits the acceptance of the check without prejudice to your rights to the full claim. To do so, endorse the check under protest citing Section 1-207 of the Uniform Commercial Code. Make copies of the front and back of the check, and immediately send one copy to the resident with notification that he or she is still liable for the full amount. Then deposit check as normal.

4. If Checks Are Stolen, Resident Is Still Liable

If your residents prefer to send checks in the mail, protect yourself against mail fraud. One rental owner in a rural area shared that where he lives, a ring of thieves hired teenagers to steal checks out of mailboxes and cash them. After that, he told his residents he had a new rule that on the back of all checks they must write "for deposit only." This means a bank cannot simply cash a check, but must deposit the check. If a bank ignores this requirement and cashes a stolen check, the bank would be liable.

Incidentally, the rental owner discourages residents from paying their rent in cash directly. If convenience stores keep less than $40 cash in their registers, why should he have to have $1,000 or more in his pockets? Another landlord who lets residents pay him in cash was attacked because people knew that he had all that cash on him. He was asking for trouble.

To make your lease sound official, find out the section of your state law that authorizes you to charge late fees and bad-check charges. Include this information in the lease. As you point out this section to residents, make it clear that you intend to collect on time and in good funds.

VIII. GO AFTER PAYMENTS DUE EVEN AFTER RESIDENTS LEAVE

Here are some ideas for going after nonpaid rent.

1. Put a Lien on the Resident's Bank Account

The following method can be used anytime after receiving a judgment. However, I would recommend waiting until after the resident moves before using this strategy. When the resident discovers you have frozen his bank account, he might see red and do massive damage to your rental just to get even.

Here are three suggested steps to follow (which may vary slightly from state to state):

1. Wait the stipulated number of days that the resident has to pay after the judgment has been awarded.
2. Return to the court and have the judgment stamped with an official seal and signed by the judge.
3. Take this official paper to the resident's bank and tell a bank officer you wish to place a lien on the resident's account. The bank will automatically freeze the account and award you whatever money is presently in the account.

To get the most money when the account is frozen, file the lien when you know the resident has a high balance. Call the bank before going there. Give the resident's bank account number, and ask if a check you have from the resident in the amount equivalent to what you have a judgment for will clear. If there is very little available on a certain day, it will be better to wait until a later date before going to the resident's bank to file the lien. Most people are paid on Friday, so calling first thing Monday morning might offer the best opportunity to file a lien and get the most money. Get in the habit of making a copy of all residents' checks every six months so you always have updated account numbers.

2. Use the Resident's License Plate Number

Photograph vehicles that your residents have and include the license plate in the picture. Make sure the letters or numbers can be read. If you have to chase down a resident who skips out, knowing the license plate number may help to locate him.

There's nothing suspicious or abnormal about taking pictures of rental property. Just make sure the cars are there and that the license plates are clearly visible.

3. Make a Phone Call or Write Letters to an Emergency Contact

A brand-new landlord met me and listened to my presentation during the apartment owners trade show and convention at the Los Angeles Convention Center. He told me the investment he's made in my newsletter and complete set of landlord resource materials has already paid for itself with just one idea. Here's what he said: "I rented a condominium to a young couple who ran into financial trouble very early into the second month of their rental term. I tried to work with them for almost eight months to catch up on their deposit and monthly payments, but to little avail. I granted them an early lease termination and they left owing me $1,271.55. I didn't feel too bad and the unit re-rented fairly soon thereafter.

"But I'm not one to give up on a deadbeat. Very conciliatory letters went back and forth and, within 11 months, I recovered $400 and lots of promises to be paid in full. I wanted to end the hassle once and for all, so I took the advice you gave to look back at the original application they filled in. I decided to see if the person listed as an emergency contact could be brought into play. [When rent is not paid, *that* is an emergency.] The parents of the daughter were listed as the emergency contacts. So, I decided to play on the parents' sense of responsibility to their 20-something daughter's plight.

"I sent a letter to the daughter in care of the parents' address. To strengthen the impact of the letter, I gave notice that nonpayment of rent would be reported to all three major credit bureaus. I also included copies of the promissory letters their daughter had sent to me with all of her sad stories. The U.S. mail delivered the pack via 2nd day priority mail (for emphasis). Lo and behold, within 72 hours of sending it, I received a call from the concerned mother. Within one week, a check came to satisfy her daughter's debt for the outstanding balance of $871.55. Case closed! Thanks for the idea!"

Note: On your rental applications, include a statement that gives you authorization to contact references, including emergency contacts, for rental consideration and collection, if necessary.

4. Call the Friend, Relative, or Person on the Applicant's Reference List

You almost always find money (some change residents left behind) in every rental that becomes vacant. When someone keeps the keys or disappears with rent still due, even a single penny left behind can be used to your advantage. I call the resident or a friend, relative, or reference listed on the application and say that "money" had been left behind and I wanted to reach the resident. At this point, the friend may immediately call the long lost resident and say, "Hey John, you'd better get this!"

Have the resident arrive at a specific time to pick up that money that you've sealed in an envelope, but don't tell him how much money has been found. If the resident left with payments due, take this opportunity to deliver a legal notice, judgment, garnishment, summons, or other document that may help you recover lost income.

5. Garnish Income Taxes

Garnishing state income tax returns is an overlooked method for collecting overdue rent money. The procedure is permissible in several states and worth considering before totally giving up on the idea of going after the money due you.

This procedure varies from state to state. Contact the supervisor of the Income Withholding Unit in your state to learn if you can garnish state income tax returns and how to proceed.

6. Use Credit-Reporting Agencies to Help Motivate

Use credit-reporting agencies to help collect money you've written off as uncollectible. Maybe not immediately, but down the road, residents may want clean up their credit records. If you've put negative marks on their reports, they'll have to pay you to clear the records. Once you obtain a judgment for rent or damage owed, putting it on the residents' credit history for seven to ten years makes it collectible for all that time.

7. What to Do If You Won a Judgment but Can't Collect

Have you lost your excitement because, despite your best collection efforts, a resident still has not paid you? Have you won a judgment in small claims court? Get excited about one more tactic. According to Jim Martin, president of The Judgment Enforcement Center, many people use debtor's examinations to get their money—some successfully and some not. People may lie to you and even to a judge, but they think twice about lying to the IRS. Jim suggests taking an IRS form 4506 (available at the IRS Web site, *http://www.irs.gov*) whenever you go to court with former residents for a debtor's exam. The judge will order them to sign IRS form 4506 if you ask. This gives you the right to see income tax reports from the previous year, directly sent by the IRS, for a $20 charge. Although the tax return information will be a year old, most people keep the same bank accounts and so on.

Did you know you could pull individuals and businesses in for a debtor's exam if you believe them to be in control of at least $250 that is owed to your debtor? This includes relatives, employers, friends, neighbors, and others. If you're a thorn in the sides of the debtor's friends, they may pressure him or her to pay up. Doing this provides another way to get moved to the top of the debtor's "payback next" list.

What is a debtor's payback next list? Because debtors usually owe a lot of people, they often rank creditors they pay back based on how much pain and suffering they cause. So do things in waves that will get you ranked number one on that list! It usually takes one trip to the courthouse. You can order your debtor to bring to the examination documents that might be used to pay off the debt. To make sure they bring the list, file a Subpoena Duces Tecum order along with your Order for Examination. (The court should have forms for both and the court clerk can make sure you're filling them out correctly.)

It also prevents them from saying, "I don't know," to everything you ask. Ask for documents (showing current employer and banking information) that help you find residents if they've taken off. Good sources are current lenders because they keep tabs on their customers.

In most states, if not all, the debtor's examination triggers an automatic lien on the debtor's personal property. Although much of the debtor's personal property will be exempt, doing this still puts another thorn in their side. Having a personal property lien also keeps them from putting assets in someone else's name to hide assets. This is called fraudulent conveyance, which can be a serious charge.

the element of aggravation and everything our debt moved up on your debtor's payback ut.

8. Final Option—Forgive What the Resident Owes

Periodically, as you review your accounts receivable, instead of getting upset about money owed, "give" the gift of forgiveness to residents who can't or won't ever pay. The process of forgiving money owed is simple and should be handled legally.

First, notify the delinquent resident with a note like this:

> Failure to make payment will result in the appropriate proceedings required by law if the payment due is not received by _____ (specific date). Failure to make payment may result in the following consequences:
>
> 1. IRS may require payment of taxes on the amount presently owed.
> 2. IRS could file charges for income tax evasion resulting in fines and/or imprisonment.
> 3. Agencies such as the Department of Public Welfare and Social Security Administration may stop any benefits you are receiving and file charges of fraud resulting in fines and/or imprisonment.

Second, file the IRS form 1099c Misc. Fill in the amount the resident owes that you are forgiving in the "nonemployee" compensation box. Inform ex-residents that unless you hear from them within a specified time, you'll send copies of the form to the IRS, Dept. of Public Assistance, Social Security Administration, and the resident. Also file with the IRS the 1099 Transmittal Form, which tells the IRS how many different people to which you sent 1099s forms.

Finally, mark your accounts receivable file for each forgiven resident "Forgiven as of ____ (date)." Should residents contact you after the fact, tell them you forgave their debts and were required by law to notify the government or face fines and/or imprisonment. Be sure to keep the paperwork on file.

TEN REASONS *NOT* TO FEEL GUILTY ABOUT COLLECTIONS AND EVICTIONS

1. Always start evictions immediately. If residents need extra time, the court will give it to them.
2. You don't make a profit with evictions. You only cut your losses.

3. You've already supplied the "needy" resident with free housing. You've done your charity work; give someone else a chance.

4. If the resident doesn't have a friend or relative to help out, doesn't that say a lot about the resident's character?

5. If anyone asks you how you could put residents out on the street, ask that person to pay the rent for them and you won't evict them.

6. Delinquent residents have illegally kept possession of your house and are stealing from you. They have stolen your home, utilities, your hard-earned investment, and your services. They are thieves. Do stores let customers go in and take from them?

7. Letting residents stay in your property when they're not paying rent is like giving them your charge card or a blank check and saying, "Feel free to spend it, because I really don't care. I like lending money interest-free, even if I'm not sure I'll get paid back."

8. How would you feel if you worked all week and your employer said he didn't have a paycheck for you? Guess what? Your resident has just told you that! Do you work for nothing?

9. If you want to give your rental away or provide free rent, you should be the one who decides who gets it, not the resident. There are a lot of people more deserving.

10. Your resident is taking money that stops you from providing for your family's needs. Sadly, some residents live better lifestyles than their landlords do. It's easy when landlords let them live rent-free! Picture yourself telling your children you couldn't give them what they wanted because you had to cover a stranger's rent, and that stranger is buying gifts for his or her children.

"It's after the first of the month! Do you know where all your rents are?"

CHECKLIST

Keep this summary review of the key points handy!

✓ The recommended way to collect rent is to set up an automatic payment plan.

✓ Don't send friendly reminder letters *after* the due date; your residents will abuse your niceness.

✓ State the date when rent is due in your lease.

✓ State in your lease when the eviction process will begin if a resident defaults.

✓ Put all requirements and penalties regarding rent in writing, always.

✓ Most landlords accept personal checks, but you're within your rights if you only accept money orders, cashiers checks, or certified funds (or any other payment method) as long as you enforce your policy equally.

✓ It's not your job to determine if residents have "good excuses." An excuse is an excuse, and if you don't treat all residents equally, you're asking for trouble.

✓ Follow what your lease says. Don't put out idle threats stressing the importance of timely payments; strict enforcement of your penalties will stress the importance far more than anything you can say. Actions speak louder than words!

✓ Make sure you enforce all rules you establish and impose any penalties you elect to use.

✓ Don't be afraid or feel guilty to take rent by force (by legal force only).

8

MAXIMIZE YOUR
CASH FLOW

*"Always ask prospective residents if they would like
'fries and a drink' with their rental."*
—JEFFREY TAYLOR

I promote a revolutionary strategy guaranteed
to improve your cash flow and upgrade the quality of residents you attract. In fact, it can totally change the way you rent and maintain your
properties. Reread these ideas more than once until light bulbs begin
exploding in your head. They're based on an evolving trend that goes
unnoticed by 95 percent of all landlords.

Today's rental residents seem to be more discriminating in their
home selections than in previous decades. Why? More apartment communities offer housing extras, features, amenities, services, and guarantees that make a standard rental seem mediocre. If you own single-family
homes as well as small multifamily buildings, you may think that because you rent houses, you have a marketing advantage over apartment
owners. Why? Because people prefer to rent houses instead of apartments. Therefore, you believe it's not necessary to offer extras. The
house is enough, right? Wrong!

Apartment communities are now smartly educating residents about
the added value of living in them over single-family or small multifamily
houses that offer nothing extra. Because of marketing, economic, and
social changes in our society, housing consumers no longer view renting

as a lesser or transitional lifestyle. Rather, it's becoming an accepted, preferred, and permanent lifestyle choice.

I. EDUCATE RESIDENTS ABOUT BENEFITS OF LEASING

Look at how the viewpoint on owning cars has changed. Americans are being sold on the idea that leasing cars has advantages over owning them. Consumers who want the features and lifestyle of a new car can arrange to have it on a limited budget and with low up-front cash.

That trend now applies to housing. New generations of renters are bombarded with advertising about features and amenities for their home environments along with optional services that go beyond their budgets. Smart apartment owners promote the fact that they can provide desired features (e.g., fitness center, tennis courts, swimming pool, spa, etc.) at much less than the cost of ownership. This appeals to renters who want immediate luxuries. It eliminates their worry of maintenance or possibly losing money should they move because of job transfers or other significant changes.

In today's mobile society, people don't stay in the same place for long. Renting provides freedom and an appealing low-cost alternative to home buying preferred by residents who want to shed the worries of home ownership. Plus, if they want the security of owning a home, they can find landlords willing to sign long-term leases at reduced rates with options to extend the term or buy.

One of my target markets includes educated renters of the future who want more than a standard rental house. Plus, if renters ever receive a tax deduction or credit for rent paid, homeowners can't gloat about that advantage any more. (Did you notice I've been selling you on the idea of renting? Use these ideas when talking to prospects and you'll fill your vacancies faster.)

This is both great news and bad news for landlords. The great news: More renters are around to fill homes and apartments. The bad news: They expect more. So if you want to continue receiving top rents, you're smart to offer value. Test the strategies that follow.

II. OFFER CUSTOM RENTAL HOME PACKAGES

1. Offer a Standard, Customized, or Deluxe Package

I suggest asking prospective and renewing residents if they'd prefer your standard, customized, or deluxe rental package. (Most landlords offer one package—standard, which includes heating, clean walls, running water, and working toilets. No extras, no frills.) Please grasp the beauty of this question. Even without saying what the various packages may include, residents think, "Wow, this guy has more than the average landlord." In fact, offering different options is more important and profitable than simply including a few extras as part of your normal rental. By packaging my rentals with a special name, I add value to whatever I include, even if it's only a used refrigerator, kitchen curtains, and a ceiling fan.

Never again "throw in" rental items as part of your standard rental. Instead, include bonuses in your rental packages, such as ceiling fans, miniblinds, curtains, choice of paint color, refrigerator, microwave, washer-dryer hook-up, maintenance guarantee, reduced rate at nearby gym, and so on.

In the first package option, the standard rental package, you'd include what you must provide by law (four-lead-paint-free walls, running water, working toilet, etc.). The deluxe package would include five to ten rental extras, services, or guarantees offered from $100 to $200 more than the standard monthly rental. Your cost would range from 25 to 50 percent of the added cash flow. The custom package would let residents select two to three of the extras included in the deluxe package. They'd pay only $20 to $60 above the standard rental rate for this package.

As you begin offering three different packages, you'll discover that few if any residents select the deluxe package, but by having this high-priced alternative, you'll whet the appetites of those who'd benefit from the customized package. When presenting your options using the supersize it strategy, a good percentage of people will want more than the standard package. This means you'll receive a boost of $20 to $60 a month per rental.

Showing prospects a list of upgrades and features included in the deluxe package is only part one of your packaging strategy. As you ask them what they'd like, discuss each upgrade individually. Watch their eyes get bigger as you discuss certain features. At least one, two, or even three upgrades will stimulate their interest and they'll choose the customized package.

2. Supersize It

I like the challenge of seeing how I can apply profit-building strategies used by other industries to the rental business. For example, landlords can learn from how the fast food industry substantially increases its cash flow. Picture a prospective customer approaching the counter at a fast food chain as the manager stands behind the counter. The customer asks for a hamburger, so the smart manager says, "Would you like fries and a drink with that hamburger?" If the customer asks for a combo package of burger, fries, and small drink, what would the manager ask? "Would you like to supersize it?"

Because the purpose of that question is to increase profits, fast food workers are trained to offer additional items or bigger packages. By simply asking, they know a significant percentage of customers will accept their offer. The supersize-it strategy works!

On a typical rental showing, a rental prospect looks at a home. She likes what she sees and says she wants it. If you're a typical landlord, you quickly pull out an application and tell her how much money it costs, including rent, application fee, and security deposit. But that's like a fast food manager responding to the hamburger-buying customer by saying, "That will be 99 cents." Nothing more. Don't fail to ask your prospect if she'd like "fries or a drink with that." Supersize it.

How? Instead of immediately asking for money, say, "I'm glad you like this home. It's our standard rental unit. However, many of our residents like that we've added upgrades and customized their homes. Can I tell you about the three to five most popular upgrades available to all new residents?" Their response is always yes.

Then show a sheet of paper that lists the upgrades—a ceiling fan, water-filter system, microwave, exterior motion light, washer and dryer, etc. (Because the popularity of items differs from city to city, conduct surveys of your current residents to see which ones appeal most in your area.) Whatever items you offer, say that all upgrades are included in the deluxe rental package that they can request for an additional $150 a month.

Chances are you're chuckling. You know that, realistically, no one will go for the deluxe package. It's more than they can handle. I realize this, but follow this order of questions.

After your prospect says she doesn't want all the items, say she can choose any one or two items ("fries and a drink") as a customized package for just $25 or $45 extra a month. If you use this supersize-it strategy consistently, one out of three prospects goes for this customized offer. You've just supersized your rental and your cash flow while increasing the chances that your resident will stay in your property longer than just one year.

Learn from the restaurant industry. Don't just ask for the money; ask if they want "fries and a drink" and see this strategy supersize your cash flow. You'll find that 20 to 50 percent of new or renewing residents take you up on your customized offers.

How Much Extra to Charge

When determining how much extra to charge in your packages, strive to cover the cost of the upgrades you provide within the first 3 to 6 months. For example, if you add a ceiling fan that costs $29.95, it would take $10 in additional monthly rent for 3 months to cover your cost. More expensive items may take 6 months to cover the cost. Remember, you want to keep the total monthly amount added to the rent a seemingly low figure to increase the likelihood of residents wanting the customized package. But even if it takes you 12 months to break even, you'll come out ahead in these four ways:

1. You've increased the income the property brings in, which adds tenfold to the value of the property and means thousands of dollars to you.
2. It's more likely you've attracted someone who will appreciate and take care of your property.
3. You've increased the probability that they'll stay long term, thus reducing your turnover costs and increasing your profits.
4. When a resident does move, you have an upgraded rental that rents for an upgraded amount.

3. Supersize It and Section 8

Will the supersize-it strategy work with Section 8 rentals? One landlord found that many in the local housing administration may give negative responses, saying that Section 8 won't pay more because of added amenities. However, all housing offices are given certain allowances for variation from designated rent formulas. If a landlord can demonstrate higher rates for comparable properties with certain amenities, Section 8 officials could approve an increase. Test it!

4. Aim to Rent More Than a Standard Home

If you and I both own similar rental homes in the same town on the same street, chances are great that my residents will stay twice as long as yours. Why? Because I have offered my residents a custom home instead of another standard rental.

But while getting more money is great, my goal with this strategy is not just about increasing income. I have a second (perhaps more important) reason for using this custom-home-upgrade strategy. I want residents to perceive, feel, and think this is more than a standard rental. That's why I introduce the concept when I first meet applicants and they look at my property. I say that they're seeing a standard rental home or apartment, but that I offer optional upgrades, so they can move into a customized home with upgrades that best meet the needs of their family.

Why is this concept so important? Because if your residents think they're only moving into a standard home, a year later (or before) they

---

Adding **V**alue for **Y**our **R**esidents

Try the following strategy when showing a vacant property to prospective residents. Say the home used to be a standard rental home, but you customized it by adding one or two upgrades (e.g., ceiling fan, etc.). Ask if they'd like you to keep the previously added upgrades for an additional small monthly amount ($10) above the standard rental price. Because this seems to be a no-brainer, most of them say, "Sure, keep them." You've just added to your cash flow and added value.

have no incentive to stay. They believe they can easily find another standard home or apartment. However, if your residents believe they're residing in a custom home with upgrades they requested or approved, they're less likely to move. In fact, they tend to stay twice as long.

Why not benefit from this powerful concept?

III. SYSTEMATICALLY REMIND RESIDENTS THAT THEY CAN RENT MORE

Like most people in America, you're probably deluged with letters, flyers, or advertisements from companies with which you've done business. Why do these companies send you something so often? Because they want you to buy more. Many business owners don't remind their customers when it's time to buy again, but the smart ones do.

You can invite, encourage, or remind residents that it's time to buy again or rent more. No, I'm not talking about sending out renewal notices once a year and raising the rent. Follow the lead of other businesses. For example, if you bought something from your favorite clothing store, a smart store manager would extend an enticing offer for you to buy again. The company where I often buy suits systematically sends me a letter every quarter reminding me of great items available. Why? Because I'm one of its preferred customers. Its flyers emphasize: More value from ____ or Don't miss this big opportunity.

Likewise, you'd invite or remind your preferred residents—what I call my 3-Star Residents—at least every six months that you want to meet all their housing-related needs and offer them more value in their rental home. Tell them it's time to add something they desire that you can provide. For example, offer a piece of exercise equipment (an item gaining in popularity) that you buy at a discount and provide as part of an increased rent. Or offer a computer for a child to use for schoolwork.

When you systematically offer additional items or services to your 3-Star Residents, you recover the up-front costs of any upgrade/service within three to six months. After that, you're receiving a profit every month. If just 20 percent of your residents take advantage of your invitation, you'll increase your cash flow *and* your residents will be happier.

Set Up a Win-Win Situation

The key to using this "reminder to rent more" strategy is to systematically communicate with residents and make sure it's a win-win situation. If I can buy exercise or computer equipment (new or used in good condition with a warranty) at a deep discount—$200 to $250 an item—then provide it for only $40 or $45 a month, this is a win-win situation. Individuals normally pay about $600 to $1,000 to buy the exercise equipment or computer system on their own, or pay two to three times more than what you charge to rent them. Also, when offering equipment (or anything that can break down because of misuse or neglect), have a rent-to-own program. Tell residents that after three years, the equipment becomes theirs. And because they will own it, ask if they agree to be responsible for their own technical support and repair maintenance. This way, residents take care of these items and it eliminates service calls to you.

Reminding residents that "it's time to take advantage of more" applies to more than offering property upgrades. Use this concept when reminding residents of your payday payment plan offer and other Mr. Landlord strategies, including your free property upgrade referral program. The point is that you never make an offer only once (whatever your offer is). Don't just hope residents will remember your offer and contact you. Instead, remind them every three to six months.

IV. HELP RESIDENTS BUY BEYOND THEIR HOUSING NEEDS

In an emerging trend, rental residents and homebuyers are being offered deals on cars, appliances, insurance, home office equipment, long-distance phone services, and even household products through their landlords or real estate agents. Landlords develop business relationships with companies that offer services and items, receiving a rebate or commission on the sales referred through them.

Real estate companies are joining this trend because it creates new profit centers while offering custom packages to consumers. Similarly, smart landlords are offering more than the standard package. Be ready

Unlimited **I**deas *for* **E**xtra **C**ash **F**low

With a lot of money being spent on finding and keeping customers, it's time to focus on maximizing the amount of income you can generate from your relationships with residents. Don't limit your income possibilities to only rental income.

Consider working deals with companies in your area to offer residents "extra" services or products beyond their housing needs. Here are some ideas:

- Work with your insurance agent to offer resident insurance.
- Contact a car dealership about promoting its specials to your residents. The dealer should be glad to give referral bonuses on new business you send.
- Make arrangements with local furniture rental centers and suppliers of office equipment in response to the growing popularity of home offices.
- Talk with your cable company about offering a special bulk-service deal to your residents. You'd be compensated for this directly by the cable company and indirectly through higher rents.
- National long-distance telephone companies will pay you a commission for signing up interested residents.
- You can even participate with national consumer direct marketing companies that residents can join to purchase their household or personal care items; in turn, you'd receive commission checks on your residents' monthly purchases. I receive thousands of dollars of added monthly cash flow every year by participating in such programs.

to offer residents a custom home package consisting of upgrades, *plus* products and services.

Offer Rent Payment Options

Offer residents a few options for paying their rents. It's a little-known secret that some residents prefer to pay biweekly—every two weeks—instead of monthly. I'm not talking about a problem scenario when residents can't come up with the rent on the first of the month and you reluctantly accept two payments. I'm talking about asking all prospective, current, and renewing residents if they'd prefer to pay biweekly or monthly.

Talking with aggressive-minded landlords using this tactic, I learned that 10 to 20 percent of their residents prefer to pay biweekly. Of course, for the privilege of paying rent biweekly, add 3 to 5 percent (or whatever works for you and your residents) to the monthly rental rate. For example, if the normal rent is $600 when paid monthly, let the resident pay $315 every two weeks. This works because some residents manage their rent payments best by paying a portion from each biweekly paycheck before

The Magic of Biweekly Payments

I can picture you're about to explode with excitement, figuring which residents will prefer this option and thereby add thousands of dollars to your annual cash flow. Or possibly you're shaking your head thinking that no residents will go for this. Test the idea by adding this question to your application before you meet another applicant: Do you prefer to make rental payments biweekly or monthly?

I guarantee a few qualified applicants will prefer the biweekly option. Also understand that those who are paying biweekly no longer have a month-to-month agreement; legally they have a biweekly agreement. Biweekly payments are *not* partial payments; they're considered payment in full. If a payment is late and you'd normally charge a late fee, you'd charge a late fee in this case. Or if payment isn't made, you'd start eviction for nonpayment. In both cases, you'd take action just like you would if a monthly rental payment wasn't made.

"Wait, Mr. Landlord. I've been accepting biweekly payments for years, and it's increasing my cash flow! But don't tell other landlords because my residents think I'm offering a unique service." That's the response I got from one landlord after I started sharing this secret. In fact, I've received tips from landlords nationwide who "came out of the closet" admitting they'd been offering residents three rental payment options: monthly, biweekly, or weekly. It's not unique but it works! Not only does it add to your cash flow, but it helps fill vacancies faster because it's perceived as unique to applicants who prefer to pay rent biweekly.

it gets spent on other items. With biweekly payments, you'd receive $315 every two weeks instead of $600 monthly. That's an extra $30 monthly, or $360 a year.

In addition, you'd receive 26 biweekly payments during the course of a 52-week year, equal to 13 months' rent. That means you'd receive an extra $630 on top of the other $360 extra rent, increasing your cash flow by nearly $1,000. If your normal rents are higher, obviously that means even more in annual income to you. That's why it's to your advantage to

---

An Extra $1,000 a Year per Resident

One Florida landlord I'll call Mr. K started offering weekly payment options to prospective residents so he could fill his vacancies by having a unique payment plan. The strategy worked! He filled his vacancies, and then discovered the icing on the cake. His cash flow jumped 20 percent because of residents who preferred to pay weekly. Instead of collecting $4,200 in rent over the year, he collects $5,200 from each resident. Yes, this is a true story! This totals an extra $1,000 a year for every resident by offering rental payment options and doing a bit more bookkeeping. With 18 residents paying weekly, he has added $18,000 to his annual cash flow! To top it off, he says, "I actually have better success getting rental payments from weekly residents than those under the monthly rental plan."

I challenge you to start asking all residents which payment plan they prefer: monthly, biweekly, or weekly. What do you lose by asking? Nothing—and potentially you gain a lot! You might be wondering, "What if residents figure it out?" I guess you're concerned that a resident may realize they're paying a lot more and want to change back. Not a problem. In fact, I suggest you clearly inform residents up front that more rent is paid for those selecting the payday or weekly plan. To ease concerns, reassure residents that you want them to select the plan that best meets their needs. Let them know that if they start with one particular plan and they want to change anytime during the rental term, they can switch as long as they give you 30 days' notice. You will find that residents who pay biweekly or weekly rarely switch to the monthly plan, while those paying monthly will switch if times get a little tough. Let residents know that they're never locked into any one plan; you want them to have their choice.

give residents choices, let them have it their way, and ask if they'd prefer to pay biweekly or monthly. Once residents agree to the payday payment plan, your goal will be to have these payments collected with one of the automatic payment plans previously discussed.

VI. REVIEW LEASING TERMS

You can get creative, too, with the terms of the lease you set up. Test the following ideas.

1. Charge an Application Fee to All Prospective Residents

In addition to any deposit you require, charge an application fee of $10 to $25 (check local statutes for any limits), which can be refundable or nonrefundable. This compensates you for time showing a rental and verifying the information in the application. When you do a credit check, getting an application or credit check fee covers your expenses. Plus, it helps eliminate future deadbeats who promise to pay but don't.

2. Require Maximum Security Deposits

Check state laws for the maximum amount allowed for a security deposit or charge the most the market will bear if there is no limit. As soon as you receive rents, fees, and deposits, put them into an interest-bearing bank account. The more time you leave the money in the account before it's spent or returned, the more interest you accumulate. Begin charging rent on the agreed-on move-in date of the agreement or when the resident actually moves in, whichever happens first. At the time you accept the application, set a day the agreement will start and the rent "meter" begins. If you aren't clear, some residents will take their time moving in and mistakenly expect not to be charged until they actually do.

3. Supersize Your Cash Flow in Reverse

Here's how one landlord reverses my supersize-it leasing strategy. He advertises an apartment with everything (refrigerator, parking, storage room, etc.) and his asking rent reflects these extras. When he gives people details about the apartment, he says they can deduct $X if they don't want the refrigerator and deduct $Y if they don't want the parking, etc. Most people accept some options. See if this strategy works in your area.

4. Rent Rooms Individually to Nonrelated Singles with Separate, Independent Leases

By renting out rooms in your house or apartment rather than the unit itself, it's possible to generate 50 percent more income than you would renting the same amount of space to a traditional family. (Check zoning restrictions related to maximum number of nonrelated occupants.)

5. Create an Accessory Apartment (Self-Contained Dwelling Unit)

By adding a toilet and sink to a room, you may be able to separate a portion of the total dwelling unit and rent to a roomer, while continuing to rent the main living space as a complete unit. (Most locales will allow this as long as cooking appliances are not provided in the accessory unit. Check with your local zoning department.) Or you could convert garages into bedrooms, using the new space as a large dwelling unit or accessory apartment.

6. Offer Seasonal Leasing

Offer short-term (e.g., three months) leases for a higher-than-normal monthly premium during a preferred time of year for your area (e.g., winter in Sun Belt states).

7. Create Executive Suites

Go all out and provide not only furniture but everything that's needed including bed sheets and silverware. Rent the dwelling for a high daily premium to a business in need of temporary short-term housing for visitors and executives.

8. Rent Detached Garages Separately from the Standard Rental Package

If one resident doesn't need garage space, rent it to a nonresident as storage space. By charging even $50 a month, you can earn an extra $600 a year. In areas where there are parking shortages, rental amounts for parking spaces on a property could considerably increase your potential income. If you decide to rent out nonliving space to nonresidents, clearly state in the leases to residents what's excluded in the rental agreement so they won't assume differently.

9. Provide Laundry Equipment

Coin-operated laundry facilities should break even with at least three-unit buildings; anything bigger should produce a profit. Good will and long retention make it even more worthwhile in a three-unit building. One set of facilities should serve up to eight units adequately. Consider adding vending machines, too.

10. Convert a Basement Room into a Storage Area

Either add to the monthly rental rate charges or make the space an optional extra. Let the resident have the option of paying an extra monthly fee for the additional space. In multiunit buildings, look around for unused space including hall closets in common areas, crawl spaces, etc. Convert these spaces into locking storage spaces and charge a monthly fee.

11. Rent Parking Space

For parking space, off-street parking, or covered parking (carport), charge $10 to $25 (or more) a month, depending on supply and demand.

12. If Your Vacant Land Is Commercially Zoned, Rent Space to Businesses for Billboards or Other Advertising

Here's how one landlord rents her land. She has a piece of property with a building that she used as a place of business. She also has two extra lots. A phone company wanted to put up a cell tower and asked to lease a 40-by-40-foot patch of weeds at the rear of the property for 25 years. By agreement, the rent for these "weeds" would increase every five years. This landlord has received only one call in three years—residents asking to direct-deposit their lease payment. With no mortgage on this land and adjacent homes, the profit from this property has provided funds for her to "live nicely" spending winters in Florida.

VII. NEGOTIATE FOR ADDITIONAL INCOME

1. Negotiate with Prospects

Before you set your rental rate, ask prospective residents the following two questions when talking to them over the phone. Their answers may get you to adjust the monthly rental price that you are in the process of establishing. Note: If you don't assume how much people are willing to spend, you may find they'll pay more than what you have in mind.

1. How much are you looking to spend on the next rental home that meets your needs?
2. How much monthly rent are you paying at your current residence?

Ask these questions as part of your market research, prior to setting your price, so that you have feedback from prospective customers *before* you determine how much rent you'll charge. When responding to residents who give you feedback over the phone, simply say that you either have something in their price range or you don't.

Once you set the rental price at the *first* showing of the rental home, *that* becomes the price. Don't change your price from that point forward and never quote different prices to different applicants.

2. Negotiate with Lenders

Use these tips when negotiating with lenders:

- When shopping for a mortgage, negotiate to make sure the bank/company pays interest on any escrow accounts.

- Use or obtain long-term mortgages to lower your monthly payments. Talk with your mortgage company about extending your shorter-term mortgages from 10 or 15 years to 30 years. Consider long-term loans when first purchasing properties.
- When negotiating for purchase and the seller is taking back a mortgage, include a clause that gives you the right to prepay the mortgage at a discount if you decide to pay it off early and in full. This way, you pay less for the property after you've already bought it. At the very least, ask for the right to match any offer of a third party who offers to buy the mortgage at a discounted amount before the maturity of the loan.
- Include a clause in the purchase agreement that gives you, the buyer, the right to collect all back rents due at the time of settlement. Explain to the seller that if he has not collected the money due by the settlement, the chances of collecting it late are unlikely. And because you're accepting the property with the deadbeat resident and all the risks involved, tell the seller the money still owed can be used as leverage to help get the resident out. (This resident will probably cause you loss of income anyway.) The seller will either go along with this reasoning or try to collect from the resident before settlement. Either way it would be good for you.

VIII. IMPLEMENT COST-SAVING MANAGEMENT AND MAINTENANCE PRACTICES

Certainly you can improve cash flow by not incurring extra costs. Try these ideas:

- Take prompt and maximum advantage of lease expiration dates. When you have the opportunity to raise rents, do so. Many landlords let months, even years, go by before realizing rents haven't been raised.
- Use an answering machine or voice mail. Ensure important calls are not lost and unimportant ones won't distract you or persist during inappropriate hours.
- Keep good records of expenses, damages, and supplies most frequently needed.

- Collect as much deposit as legally possible. And collect as much as your market can bear so you have leverage with residents to leave in a cooperative manner.
- Do semiannual inspections of your properties.
- Reduce vacancy make-ready time. Train someone or hire a professional to get a vacancy ready and show it within the shortest possible time. For do-it-yourself landlords, create and follow a checklist.
- Get nonpaying residents out fast. If you see that some residents have no plans to pay or move out voluntarily (which likely means a drawn-out court scenario), bribe them with promising their deposit money (to which they probably aren't entitled) to help with their moving expenses. Offer this in exchange for an agreement to move out by a designated day, leaving the property in acceptable condition. Don't pay promised funds until residents have moved out. This strategy can save you loads of frustration as well as lost income.
- Charge for completing a loan-verification sheet. When residents buying a new home apply for mortgages, charge them a fee for filling out a loan-verification sheet. I keep the faxed verification in the residents' files. (Many professional managers usually charge $25 for this verification.)
- Take every tax allowance permitted by law for rental property owners and real estate investors. Talk with your accountant about the details.

IX. CUT EXPENSES

Try these ideas to cut expenses:

- Purchase your supplies from the same hardware store and ask for discounts. Hardware stores seldom voluntarily inform you that you can set up an account and receive a 10 percent (or more) discount on all purchases. Build buying power by purchasing as many supplies as possible from the same store (even if you just own a duplex).
- Use the same color paint on all interior walls. Buy paint in large quantities and store it where it won't spoil.
- Check the Web sites of your favorite stores (for building supplies and materials) to obtain discount coupons (for example, Lowes

and Home Depot offer discount coupons that can save you hundreds of dollars) when you move to a new property.

- Use a master lock system. This helps rekey present locks when residents move out, and saves time and money changing locks.
- Purchase appliances at wholesale or discount prices and sell them to residents. Don't include appliances as part of the rental agreement. If you already have them, tell residents you will sell them at a low price and buy them back when they move out (if they want). When residents own the appliances, they take better care of them. And if they break down or need repair, the landlord isn't responsible to fix them.
- Reduce any utility expense. Rule of thumb: It shouldn't take more than three years to recoup the expense of all improvements made to conserve utilities. If it does, the improvement is probably not cost effective.
- Find ways to lower expenses for utilities, even if you're not responsible for paying them. That makes the property more attractive to your prospects and residents. The savings can indirectly encourage residents to stay longer. And it's easier to charge top rents if you know utility expenses won't be astronomical.
- For utilities you cover, determine the average monthly expense and set a tight but reasonable limit you'd like the bill to stay under. Then offer residents an incentive (cash rebate) for every month they use less than the stated amount.
- Install shower flow restrictions and low-flush toilets. If you have to replace a toilet, buy one that uses 3½ gallons of water or less. It's not worth the savings, however, to take out toilets with higher water usage that still work. Also, install shower stall drip stops at the corners of your showers to prevent water from splashing out.
- Install more insulation, thermal windows, and high-efficiency furnaces when replacements are necessary.
- Turn off the pilot to the gas heater during the five warmest months.
- Negotiate a volume discount from a local oil dealer. Get together with other owners (e.g., from an investment, rental, or apartment association) so you have more buying power.
- Separate heating and domestic hot water heaters and boilers. That allows you to disconnect the heating boiler during the summer and use a more cost-effective hot water heater.

- Install an insulating blanket on each water heater.
- Put a timer on the hot water circulating pumps. Have them shut down at night around midnight and come back on in the morning around 5:00 AM to save on the expense of heating hot water. Turn down the temperature settings on hot water heaters and furnace/boilers until you have complaints.
- Test the ducting system of your heating units. Properly sealing ducts have resulted in up to 20 percent energy savings for some rental owners. Have a contractor check behind registers, in crawl spaces, and/or in attics for crushed, disconnected, or leaky ducts. Repair them with mastic-type sealant, not duct tape.
- Consider replacing old windows. Windows can account for 33 percent of the total heat loss and as much as 75 percent of the heat gain in summer. That's why it's a good idea to consider installing high-efficiency windows.
- Separate residents' utilities and billing. Whenever possible—and when you can recoup your expense within three years—separate utilities so residents can be responsible for individual payment of their own utility bills. Initial costs may seem high, but worth it the first time a resident abuses the use of a utility expense.
- Check out companies offering submetering services. They're able to measure individual usage on the same master meter and then bill and collect from each resident. The premise behind this service is that residents who are aware of and responsible for usage will use less.

X. UNCOVER HIDDEN CASH FLOW THIEVES

Just as you can reduce costs through better management practices or by cutting expenses, be aware of how you can save by managing your funds carefully. Beware of these service providers who could turn out to be cash flow "thieves."

1. High-Interest Mortgage Lenders

Refinance your high-interest loan through either conventional lenders or other money sources. Even consider family or friends willing to lend you money at a low rate for you but higher return than they could get at a bank.

2. Tax Assessors

At least 20 to 33 percent of all property tax assessments are too high. If you own property in an area where values have gone down, check into the tax appeal process and learn how to appeal your assessed values. A reduction in your property tax is just like getting a rent increase.

3. Banks or Loan Companies with Adjustable Rate Mortgages

Are you making payments on an adjustable rate mortgage? Statistics from loan checking services indicate that error rates on principal recalculations run between 25 and 50 percent. Typical errors include using the wrong index value, erroneous timing on the change in index, and rounding the payments incorrectly. These errors can cost you several hundreds and even thousands of dollars.

4. Note Holders Who Require Mortgage Insurance

Once you have reduced your loan and increased your equity—or can prove with a new appraisal that your equity has increased—don't continue paying extra for mortgage insurance that's required for small equity on many loans. Banks and mortgage holders won't voluntarily tell you when you can stop paying extra monthly payments toward the insurance, even though in many contracts it clearly states when payment is no longer necessary. When negotiating for new loans and mortgage insurance is required, find out at what point it will no longer be required. If you're paying mortgage insurance now, find out how much equity you need before insurance isn't needed.

5. Utility Companies

Yes, errors are often made on utility bills—phone, water, and sewage. You may be paying the wrong rate or qualify for a lower rate. Rates are often negotiable. In fact, the problem has gotten to the point at which you can hire specialized services to audit your utility bills and let you know if mistakes have been made (or if you can obtain lower rates). They may also help you get a refund. The problems are so widespread that these companies claim they can get refunds for three out of every four clients. They often charge a percentage of the refund to which you're entitled.

Be aware that in instances when your bill is excessive due to a problem on your end (such as a broken water pipe), once the problem has been corrected, you can request a reduction or adjustment in your bill. Talk with utility company representatives when you have a problem that causes an excessive bill. Ask to be billed at a lower rate. (Many won't inform you unless you make a request.)

6. Contractors Who Delay or Switch Quality of Materials

Waiting for contractors to complete projects affects your cash flow. Always have a penalty clause (per day) in your contract for any work not completed by a designated date. Also be aware of rip-off tactics like painting and switching (for example, you're paying for a high-quality paint but a low-grade, inexpensive paint was used instead). Painters might overestimate the number of gallons required for the job, and then charge the difference. Similar tactics can be used by any contractor for any materials they verbally tell you they are buying. Always get everything in writing; don't assume anything. You may want to purchase the materials yourself.

7. Appraisers

Because of the regulation and consistency of operation in the appraisal industry, *wide* variation of prices can occur. Never assume the first appraisal is the best you can get, or the appraisal done by a mortgage company or even city-hired appraiser has to be the last word on the matter. For a few hundred dollars, get another appraisal that could show a difference of several thousands of dollars. This could help when selling or buying rental property. Always talk with other investors and find out what appraisers they've used and the type of appraisal provided. Always prepare the price you think a property is worth and reasons you selected that price to assist hurried appraisers in their jobs.

8. Insurance Companies

Insurance agents like to set you up with separate insurance policies on numerous rentals carrying a small deductible on each. Once you obtain several rentals, consider working with a company that can put all your policies into a package deal with an umbrella liability policy. Set your deductibles for the basic fire protection high, especially if you own several rentals, because the chances of something happening to one, let alone more, are low. Keep close tabs on your insurance costs. Be a nuisance to your insurance broker. Make sure you're getting the best rates available and that you understand the necessity of the policies you own.

9. Loan Services

Late charges are a multibillion-dollar income source for dishonest mortgage services that use clever schemes to increase their late charge revenue. A typical scenario would be that you mail your monthly mortgage payment to the loan service on time, but the service either waits until after the grace period before depositing it or waits before sending your check to the mortgage owner at a different location (even a different state) where it arrives past the grace period. In both cases, you get charged a late fee. Because the majority of individuals won't argue but just pay the extra charge, this practice is becoming more common. If you suspect improper charges, send your payments by certified mail with a return postal receipt requested.

XI. INCREASE PROPERTY VALUE

Increasing the perceived value of your property results in greater monthly cash flow and property appreciation. (Please note that all suggestions are intended to enhance value, not disguise faults.) Use the following suggestions as a mini-makeover for improving the appearance and appeal of your buildings—both inside and out.

1. Add Value to the Interior

- Have an industrial-strength cleaning job done on all interior surfaces.
- Repaint all walls and surfaces, and consider adding trim molding.
- Get a plasterer to put a fancy swirl pattern on the walls and ceilings in the main rooms—dining room, living room, and master bedroom.
- Replace any damaged interior doors, and replace lock sets with new ones.
- For a touch of elegance, add one or two ceiling fans.
- Replace outdated or cracked receptacle face plates and electrical switch plates. Put in fancy light switch plates and a dimmer switch for one or two rooms.
- Replace all floor coverings,   leum or vinyl flooring. Consider   ramic tile.
- Install new shower curtain and toilet seats and repair or replace bathroom faucets at tub, shower, and sink with fancier ones.
- Put up new miniblinds.
- Replace or repair chipped or blemished countertops; replace burner reflector pans.
- Reface kitchen cabinet doors or replace, and upgrade all hardware on the cabinets.
- Add a closet, cabinet, or storage space where reasonably possible.

2. Add Value to the Exterior

- A paint job can add thousands of dollars to the house's value if done by an experienced painter and with quality paint. Use color combinations that add character to your building's appearance. Consult with paint store personnel.
- Have the exterior pressure washed to remove all dirt from the surfaces. Then use trim and touch-up paint around the windows and where needed.
- Do some landscaping, including trimming trees, hedges, and bushes; mow the grass; and add silk flowers for year-round appeal in flower boxes.

- Add a decorative screen or a storm or security door. Replace the standard entry door with a decorative one. Add a fancy door knocker and a doorbell.
- Replace the mailbox with a fancier box; replace property's street address numbers with a fresher look.
- Replace outdated windows. Add window shutters to older homes. Consider replacing outmoded windows altogether. You can replace old wooden frames with aluminum frames, with plain single pane clear glass. Tinted or insulated glass does not give enough additional value to make up for their added costs.
- Replace outmoded porch light fixtures, adding inexpensive but elegant-looking ones.
- Add motion sensor lighting, or lighting that comes on at dusk and goes off at dawn.
- Clean, replace, or install gutters and down spouts.
- Remove or require all trash and litter to be removed from around the property.
- Replace or repair loose or missing roof shingles or exterior siding.
- Consider adding a fence, or repair or improve the look of the fence that's already there.

9

KEEP RESIDENTS LONG AFTER THEIR FIRST ANNIVERSARY

"Do not assume that just because you have not heard from your residents that they are happy and plan on staying another year."
—JEFFREY TAYLOR

The most successful businesses keep their customers happy and paying for their services year after year. That ability to keep customers—residents, in your case—separates the successful, happy landlords from the not-so-successful ones.

The national average for residents residing in the same rental is a little longer than one year. The average turnover costs landlords one to two months' rent because of fix up, advertising, and loss of income. *Having a vacancy can cost you between $800 and $1,500 a month or more, depending on the rents in your area.*

How can you increase the likelihood your residents will stay a minimum of three years? Let me share key resident retention principles and strategies that are amazingly simple to put into practice. Even more amazing—they're neglected by most landlords.

I. COMMUNICATE STARTING ON DAY ONE

Implement the following five communication actions.

1. Focus on Anniversary Dates, Not Renewal Dates

When prospects complete my rental applications, they see this question: Would you like to receive a gift on your anniversary date? The question itself implies that this won't be a temporary relationship but a long-term one. Naturally, most people respond by saying yes. When they do, I tell them they can take advantage of my 3-Star Resident program, and then I send an official letter announcing they're part of the program.

Once residents begin living in your rentals, the words you convey are as important as what you actually do to promote long-term relationships.

2. Convey Long-Term Customer Benefits with Your Company's Slogan

Here are a few examples of slogans you can use to communicate how you can meet the housing needs of your customer:

- "Rent from us today; buy from us tomorrow"
- "We offer more than four walls and a floor for our 3-Star Residents"
- "We reward our long-term residents"
- "Here to meet all your housing-related needs"

Of course, just saying this is not enough; you must put action behind your words.

3. Set Up a Resident Retention Program

A smart landlord begins efforts to retain residents as soon as the lease begins. Studies show that half the residents decide if they'll renew within the first seven days of living in a new residence. Consider these ideas:

- Leave a thank-you note in clear sight for residents when they move in. This gesture helps cement your relationship; people love to be courted.
- Visit residents within the first week of the lease. Show them how to use the appliances. Welcome them to their new home.

Between the fourth and sixth month, call residents and ask, "What one thing do you like best about your new home? Do you know anyone else interested in renting a nice home or apartment?" Also ask if any one thing needs to be taken care of. You want to know now, not six months later, when the resident wants to move because of a minor problem. In my experience, 70 percent of the residents have decided if they'll renew their leases by the sixth month of a lease. Put your best foot forward.

- Always smile when you're in the presence of your residents. The spotlight is on you. Place a reminder sign to smile by your phone and in your car where you'll see it on your way to visiting residents, working at rentals, and meeting prospects. Never give in to the temptation to snap back at residents when they grouch at you. After all, your behavior affects your reputation, your residents' cooperation, the longevity of your relationship, and word-of-mouth referrals. Don't let molehills become mountains.

4. Tell the Truth

At first glance, it may seem smart to hide the drawbacks of your rental or the neighborhood when first communicating with prospects. But if you don't, you're buying trouble and setting yourself up for a short-lived relationship. Tell applicants up front about any lack of parking on the street or the new highway being built nearby. Be careful not to present the information in a negative tone. Instead, project the attitude that "it's still a great place." You may lose prospective residents, but telling the truth up front prevents irate middle-of-the-night phone calls.

5. Make Your Property Communicate the Right Way

A property presented the right way will reward you with long-term dollars. What should your property be communicating?

- "I am showcase clean." Remove any reminders of previous residents in vacant rentals. Remove old kitchen paper towel hangers and leftover coat hangers from closets. Remove evidence of bathtub decals. Toss old doormats in the trash.

- "This place looks brand new!" The property should be shouting that it's fresh and ready for new residents. Put in fresh rolls of toilet paper, drinking water/cups, a brand-new doormat, a beautiful plant, and so on. Give it the never-lived-in-before look.

II. TAILOR WHAT YOU OFFER

Take these three suggestions to heart.

I. Tailor Your Anniversary Dates

Move-outs happen! That's a fact in the rental business. The trick, however, is not to have untimely move-outs in months when it's hardest to re-rent properties quickly, such as the dreadful winter months.

To eliminate wintertime move-outs, offer lease terms throughout the year that don't end during the months of December, January, or February (in most regions). Consider offering a lease term between 6 and 24 months. *You* determine when the anniversary dates occur. If your market has other seasonal slow periods, then set the lease terms to avoid anniversary dates in months that are disadvantageous to re-leasing the unit quickly.

Equally apply these principles of lease-term management to current residents renewing their agreements. Established customers are even more open to long renewal lease terms. Begin a comprehensive lease-term management program today to take control of managing your properties.

2. Tailor the Property

How can you get top-market rent and keep residents for a long time while raising rents? You do so by adding value (e.g., upgrades, improvements, or services) that appeals to your targeted segment of the population. Residents see the benefit in paying top-market rent and staying with you because your package offers features they can't get elsewhere.

3. Tailor Your Rental Increases

Don't increase rents as much for hard-to-rent units as you do for rentals in high demand.

III. PLUG YOUR RESIDENTS INTO YOUR PROPERTY

Smart landlords know that the more you make residents feel plugged into their property, the neighborhood, or your management system, the longer they'll stay. Long-term residents drastically reduce turnover costs that can negate your positive cash flow efforts while adding thousands to your bottom line.

The following ways help keep residents plugged in:

- Provide a personalized doormat or welcome sign that reads: Welcome to the (residents' last name) home.
- Send a short quarterly newsletter to your residents, even if you have only one rental. Receiving communication monthly makes residents feel more connected to you, especially if it includes items of interest. For example, you could pass on grocery coupons or money-saving certificates for local businesses or restaurants. Get marketing mileage from every dollar you spend by promoting property improvements and anniversary and rental rewards in your newsletters and anniversary letters.
- Send birthday cards to residents and/or their children.
- At the beginning of the rental relationship, give residents a list of 12 possible upgrades or improvements you would do over the next three years. After each anniversary date and a satisfactory property inspection, they select one upgrade from the list. After three upgrades have been received, reward residents with part of their security deposit back.
- Give residents a special rental ID card. Work a deal with a health club, beautician, restaurant, hardware store, etc., that entitles them to a 10 percent discount by showing their ID card.

IV. OFFER LOYALTY PROGRAMS TO REWARD LONG-TERM RESIDENTS

These five programs have worked like magic for me and other landlords.

1. Develop a 3-Star Resident Program

When I first started managing my properties, a resident would normally stay one year. Now that norm is five to six years. Why? Because I've designed programs modeled after frequent-flyer programs. Their programs give me a perk for doing business with them. When I decide which store, airline, or hotel to use, those businesses with reward programs come to mind first.

Make that true for residents, too. After 10 or 11 months, most residents start wondering if they'll stay another year because they've been trained to think in yearly intervals. Average landlords even encourage that kind of thinking by asking residents if they want to renew. I say, don't let your residents *think* every year whether or not to stay with you. Instead, get them into a program that encourages them to feel connected to you.

When residents move in to one of my properties, I welcome them into my 3-Star Resident program. It doesn't cost them anything and they get perks by being a part of it. Their "anniversary" becomes a time of celebration. Every year, I give them a choice of property upgrades (costing between $25 and $75 each) for paying rent on time. Some landlords wonder why I reward people for doing what they're supposed to do anyway. I regard my residents as business partners and vital members of my success team; giving rewards helps our relationship work. It also encourages them to stay longer than one year. To avoid vacancies, I'm glad to give a property upgrade that costs $75 or less. Too many times, landlords try to be cheap and step over dollars to save nickels. This isn't rocket science; I've proven that people stay longer when I offer upgrades!

After each of the first three years as residents, they receive their choice of a property upgrade as part of my 3-Star program.

Every time I send letters, I remind them that they're 3-Star Residents. Every time someone does maintenance on the property, the person doing the work says, "Mr. Jones, I'm glad you're one of our 3-Star

Residents. We're here to provide excellent service to you." I offer my 3-Star program for three years because people can only handle three years at a time. If you offered a 5-Star (five-year) or 10-Star (ten-year) program, they'd look at you cross-eyed. After a year, residents won't think about moving because they're part of this 3-Star program. Okay, 20 percent *will* move because of job transfers or something similar. But with this simple strategy, you influence the 80 percent who would otherwise move out after only one year.

After ten months, I send letters that read: "Thank you for letting us serve you for the first year of your 3-Star program. We look forward to serving you for another two years. Please sign this so we can deliver the benefit that was promised to you at this time and continue serving you for the next two years in our 3-Star program." When they sign off for the benefit, they're signing off for another two years. Case closed. Put the letters on file.

2. Announce a VIP Program

Is there a disadvantage to the 3-Star program? Yes, it's only three years long. So in the third year, I announce a new program: the VIP program. Starting the fourth year, I return $100 of their deposit. They are happy to receive this, especially during the holiday season. And what money am I actually giving them? I say I'll give them another $100 the following year. In fact, I keep giving them $100 until the deposit is fully returned.

Some landlords say, "Wait a minute. Now you don't have money to cover yourself." Well, most residents need to stay about 12 years before they get all their money back. At that point, I'm covered because they've practically paid for the place anyway! Why, then, should you do like the average landlord and wait until residents leave to give their deposits back? Instead, reward them for their loyalty because it's not really costing you anything. Certainly by their fourth year, you're not risking much. Because of your regular inspections, you know if they're taking care of your property.

3. Redecorate Everyone's Unit

Here's a wild thought: Redecorate everyone's rental unit—that is, everyone who's been living there for two years or more. If you do, chances are they'll stay another two or three years. Landlords who've made this offer say some residents don't take them up on this offer until later because they don't want the disturbance. But knowing the offer is available to them, they no longer get angry that their rental has never been repainted and won't leave because of a penny-pinching attitude by the management.

Most residents contemplate moving when their present rental needs repainting, the drapes are dirty, the shower door is cracked, and the kitchen linoleum is wearing through. To get a fresh new lift to their life, they need to move into a freshly refurbished rental. Then all their problems will go away. Ironically, the rental they move into was probably vacated by someone else because it needed repainting.

4. Spend Now to Prevent Loss Later

What does it cost to redecorate a rental before it becomes vacant? Check the arithmetic. It costs about $150 for minor redecorating and $50 for shampooing the carpets, a total of $200. But you can spread these costs over a two-year period. Estimate your cost at $100 a year. On a $600-a-month rental, if it were vacant for two weeks while you fixed it up to attract new renters, you'd lose $300 in rent money and spend $200 to redecorate after the fact. Spend $200 over two years to prevent a $500 loss.

Suppose you're in danger of losing good renters because a new apartment building up the street has more modern kitchens than yours and you can't afford to redo your kitchens. What can you do? Rather than let good residents move, have them select a new appliance of their choice and go halves with them on the purchase. (Make an agreement that, when they move, ownership of the appliance will revert to the property or they can pay a little more and take it with them.)

I let residents pick out what they want from an appliance store (to a given dollar limit). I know they'll take care of it because they're paying for half of it. And, they won't leave soon because they've put their own cash into the kitchen. Furthermore, they're probably better off than they would be by incurring the cost of moving. I'm money ahead because the rental isn't vacant, plus I've increased its value. If other renters complain, I simply offer the same deal to them. That's always more profitable than finding people to replace them.

5. Offer Longevity Pricing

Reward long-term residents with discounted rent increases. Structure increases based on the length of time a resident has stayed. For example, residents starting their third year wouldn't receive as big of an increase as residents starting their second year.

V. REMEMBER RESIDENTS THROUGHOUT THE YEAR

Remember, you're building long-term relationships; you don't just show up when it's time to pay or renew. These five suggestions will help you strengthen your customer relations.

1. Recognize Your Residents

Compliment or recognize every resident at least once every three to six months, often through written communication. For example, put a special note in the resident newsletter. Send a holiday greeting card, an anniversary card, or a birthday card and recognize resident achievement (home of the month, yard of the month, child's graduation, etc.). Or purchase an inexpensive rubber stamp that reads "Our Residents Are Special," and stamp every piece of correspondence you send to them.

Overcome the Top Reason for Switching

According to a federal government survey, the top reason people switch services (i.e., rental housing) is because they sense indifference on the owner's part. This reason was given five times more often than "dissatisfaction with quality of service," which was the second biggest reason. This is good news for landlords. It means even if you can't provide prompt or superior service, you can always take time to recognize your residents.

2. Start a Greeting Card Campaign

Several landlords have reported renewal and occupancy rates as much as 30 percent higher by implementing a simple greeting card campaign. They send cards with colorful designs and messages such as, "We really appreciate having you as one of our 3-Star Residents, and we look forward to rewarding you on your anniversary dates." They are sent at the following times:

- 1 week after move-in
- 45 days after move-in
- 6 months after move-in
- 10 months after move-in (with an anniversary thank-you letter enclosed)

Also send cards when the home or apartment has undergone renovation. The card could say, "Thanks for hanging in there!" and let your residents know you realize the inconvenience caused by the renovation.

3. Make Random Calls

Periodically make what would appear "random" calls asking residents if there is one thing you can help them with or any one problem you can correct.

4. Remember Residents During the Holidays

Budget enough income to offer a small, one-time rent discount or gift during the holiday season. Few landlords offer extras like this, yet it shows your residents you remember them. If a small holiday gift helps keep a good resident a year longer, it's well worth extra money.

5. Spotlight a Resident

If you send a newsletter to your residents each month or quarter, consider including a "Resident Appreciation Spotlight." This consists of a few paragraphs in which you recognize and thank a selected resident.

Send Newsletters, Even When Numbers Are Small

You don't have to have a lot of residents for this newsletter idea to be effective. Even if you only have two to four rental homes, I encourage you to send out a newsletter quarterly. Use it to remind them of maintenance responsibilities, for example, preparation for winter weather. If you only have a few residents, spotlight one resident one or two months of the year.

Simply choose a resident and ask for permission to do a short write-up on him or her or on their business. Most residents appreciate the free publicity about themselves or their businesses.

VI. PLAN AHEAD FOR REPAIRS AND SERVICE

These four ideas will make sure service problems don't become headaches for you.

1. Handle Repairs and Service Calls Promptly

Set up a plan to coordinate with a contractor so that repairs and service calls can be handled promptly. Put a maintenance guarantee plan into effect. Nothing infuriates residents as much as when they feel a maintenance request gets ignored.

2. Realize That Dealing with Resident Problems Is Part of Your Business

Landlords wrongly try to cut expenses by putting off the needs of residents until it's more convenient for you or hired help. Give your residents a maintenance guarantee. Offer to handle any problem that is your company's responsibility within 72 hours or residents start getting free rent. Anything short of giving this incentive to your residents delays compensation to them and will put a strain on your landlord-resident relationship.

3. When Repairs Are Made, Don't Be a Miser

Saving pennies can cost thousands. Don't try to get by with minimal repairs when major renovation is needed. When you do, good residents feel shortchanged.

4. Provide a Maintenance Request Form at the Beginning of the Rental Term

Not only will having a request form show you're a concerned landlord, but getting specific information helps you prioritize jobs and allocate time and materials. Create a general request form that also applies to nonmaintenance situations.

VII. GO THE EXTRA MILE

To give excellent service, don't hesitate to provide extras that cement your relationships.

1. Make Move-In Day an "Extra" Good Day

Moving day is often unpleasant for residents, so get their minds thinking in the right direction. Help turn that potentially bad day into a good (at least a pleasant) one. What could you do? Contract with your

---

Don't **R**isk **D**ollars *to* **S**ave **P**ennies

Landlords lose good residents as well as income during any vacancy period. They also spend money on fix-ups to attract new residents who may or may not work out. Don't try to save pennies at the risk of losing dollars (or thousands of dollars). Instead of putting a new appliance in the empty rental, for example, give it to the resident who's been with you at least a year. Tell new residents right away that, as a reward for staying for a certain length of time, they'll receive an appliance.

local pizza company to deliver a pizza to the rental while your new residents are moving in. This has a much greater impact than simply giving them a coupon.

2. Make Five Extra Minutes Go a Long Way

The next time a maintenance person is called to make a repair in one of your rentals, after they complete the job, have them tell the resident, "Because you're a 3-Star Resident, I'll be glad to take an extra five minutes before my next appointment to help with a minor task." Most of the time, they won't take you up on the offer, but offering contributes to high resident retention. They can carry light bulbs and ask if one needs to be replaced. They can have air conditioner or furnace filters ready to be replaced, which is preventive maintenance that saves money. Have them carry caulking so they can check around the tub and touch it up. This provides an opportunity to inspect the bathroom and check if a toilet is running, which can be costly if you pay the water bill. Or they can ask residents if they need one minor thing done, like tightening a towel rack or hanging a picture. Whatever *extra* small task they perform, the gesture goes a long way toward making residents happy. And it only took an extra five minutes.

If the resident isn't home at the time of repair and a maintenance person does one "extra" little thing, leave a note saying what's been done, and then thank them for being a resident. It's like going to the bakery and getting 13 donuts instead of 12.

VIII. ANTICIPATE AND AVOID VACANCIES

Your goal is to keep your rental units occupied with quality residents. Here are three tactics to employ.

1. Send Out Mid-Lease Questionnaires

I ask residents what they'd like to have not at the *end* of their leasing year, but in the middle. Why? Because I don't want the only communication to occur when rents might be raised. Similarly, I don't want to come into contact with residents only when I pick up payments. Then they'd regard me as someone who only wants handouts.

I've run into landlords who proudly announce they haven't talked to their residents in a few years. But by not finding out how they can better serve their customers, I believe they're leaving dollars on the table. If you serve residents better than ever, you'll make more money than ever. They're happier; they stay longer; everybody wins.

2. Conduct "Pre-Anniversary" Warm-Up Calls

Call residents 60 days before sending a rent increase or anniversary letter. Confirm your residents' satisfaction and identify what you can do to secure a favorable response.

3. Influence Their Plans to Move

When residents say they plan to move, I suggest systematically responding this way:

1. Converse with the residents within two days. Speed is critical. As time passes, their decision to move becomes more irreversible.
2. Ask them their reasons for moving.
3. If they cite a rent increase as the reason, probe for other underlying issues and address them.
4. Ask about unmet needs that you could correct.
5. Offer a moving discount off the first month's rent if they move to another one of your rentals.

IX. RAISE RENTS WITHOUT SCARING GOOD RESIDENTS AWAY

Have you had good residents and didn't want to raise their rents because you didn't want them to move? I raise the rent, even on good residents. I don't worry that they might move; my residents are actually happy I've raised the rent. Here are two ways to accomplish this. Choose your favorite!

1. What Would You Consider a Fair Middle Ground?

Let's say you want a $25 increase in the rent. Send residents a letter saying, "As mentioned at the beginning of your rental term, rent will increase each year. It's about to increase in the next 60 days. The increase will be $50 every month." Remember, you only want $25, but in the letter, double the amount you want. The letter continues, "We do, however, seek to work with residents who have unique circumstances. If you are facing financial difficulty, please contact us within the next five days."

Residents will contact you, claiming financial hardship. How do you respond? Don't just ask what they can afford. Ask: "What would you consider a *fair middle* ground?" Those two words are important. Residents will find the middle and say "$25." Even if they say $20, I'll accept it and say, "I think our company can work with that." Residents feel good that they had a chance to limit the increase. And you walk away with the increase you wanted in the first place!

2. What's the Maximum Your Budget Can Handle?

An owner was afraid to raise the rent, even though she decided she could get an extra $5 to $10 a month. Then she tried this idea she read about in the *Mr. Landlord* newsletter: Before you tell a resident how much the rent is going up, approach him or her and say, "I'd like to have a discussion with you. Your anniversary date is coming up, and our company has certain expenses we have to cover. We need to raise the rent. Before we do that, because we know this would concern you, we wanted to get your feedback. We really need to go up a *lot* on the rent, but you tell us—what's the maximum your budget can handle at this time? We might be able to work with you."

After the property owner had this discussion, the resident wanted to talk it over with her husband. They came back and said, "We looked at our budget. We decided we could handle a $50 a month increase. And if we had to, we could do as much as $75 a month. But we can't handle more than that." Remember, the owner would have been happy with a $5 or $10 increase. But she didn't open her mouth; she let them talk first. She went with the $50 increase, saying, "Our company will work with you by only increasing your rent $50." The residents felt relieved; the landlady felt fantastic!

Let Them Talk!

Owners of small or large multifamily buildings are often concerned that residents will talk and compare how much rent they pay. Talking plays to your advantage, whether you have 2 or 200 residents. Apartment 1: They don't call you and their rent increases $50. Apartment 2: They call you and negotiate a $25 increase. For some landlords, this would be a problem because they only provide four walls and a floor. The two units are equal—that's where the problem is. So, within three days of sending the rent increase notice and before residents have a chance to speak with each other, if I have not heard from a resident for a rent negotiation I initiate contact to customize the home of the person paying the full $50 increase. I look at their most recent customer survey to find out what they want (e.g., a TV, a computer, etc.) and what they said they'd be willing to pay extra for. I give them this item plus perhaps something extra. Then the two residents talk. Guess who's mad? The one in the standard rental home whose rent only increased $25.

You can also tell them you're taking a smaller increase than you'd planned, so you'd like them to do a simple maintenance item they might not normally take care of. When the landlady said, "We can accept just the $50," she added, "but we will need you to trim the bushes in the front yard." The residents said, "Sure."

X. CONDUCT EXIT INTERVIEWS

In the book *Megatrends,* author John Naisbitt evaluated the future of American businesses. His premise was that the most successful businesses would have the most information. He stressed that the companies with the most knowledge of their customer, competition, and product will be winners. This certainly applies to property management.

As important as it is to gather information before residents move in, it's equally vital to collect information from residents before they move out through an exit interview. You want to learn about your product (your rental home or apartment) and why it no longer met the needs of your customer (the resident).

Conduct an interview before returning security deposits. Don't stop after you discover why the resident moved; each piece of information can help make future management more successful. Find out to where residents are moving and what about the competition attracted them. Ask what originally attracted them to your rental and determine how close you came to meeting their expectations. What would your residents add or change that would have better met their needs? Ask if they know of friends or co-workers who may be interested in your rental property.

The more information you gather through surveys and interviews, the better you can meet the needs of future residents. Conduct exit surveys before returning security deposits to increase the likelihood that they'll cooperate and let you conduct your exit interview.

These are the most avoidable reasons good residents leave (gleaned from exit surveys and interviews):

- Neglected maintenance
- Bad residents as neighbors
- Slow or nonresponsive landlord
- Lack of security or threat to the building's security
- No improvements ever done
- Perception that owner is indifferent to the concerns of the resident
- Not receiving enough value compared to what other properties are offering
- No real benefit or incentive that would make it advantageous to stay longer

Using the action steps in this step, you will not lose residents for any of those reasons. And, as you'll read in the next step, you will be one step closer to generating additional profits even after the rental relationship ends.

S *t e p*

10

END ALL RELATIONSHIPS ON A "PROFITABLE" NOTE

"Rent from us today; buy from us tomorrow."
—MIKE RUKAVINA

As rental relationships inevitably end, it's to your advantage that they always end on a positive note because you can both reap additional benefits.

Typically, here's how a rental relationship ends (but not the way I propose it should end!). Residents give/send notice to the owner/manager that they're moving. The landlord informs vacating residents to leave the property the way it was at move-in. As the landlord attempts to fill the soon-to-be-vacant rental, vacating residents don't readily make the home available for showing. When a showing is permitted, the place looks "marginal" and they even make unflattering comments about the property when the landlord is out of earshot. (Because of this, most landlords try not to show or re-rent the property until after residents move out.)

Once they vacate, the landlord inspects the premises and decides the property hasn't been left as it was at the beginning of the relationship, and consequently decides to withhold part of the security deposit. It takes several days, sometimes a week or longer, to fix all deferred maintenance problems, clean the home, and make needed improvements to get it ready to advertise and show. By the time a new resident is found and actually moves in, two to four weeks have passed. You've lost time and money because of uncooperative residents.

Clearly, this doesn't represent a win-win situation. Under this scenario, the residents end the relationship feeling unhappy and so does the landlord, who doesn't like to incur extra costs despite having kept part of the measly security deposit. (Note: Landlords are required by law to return the security deposit to the vacating resident within a certain period of days or be subject to penalty. Check your state laws for the time period requirement in your area.)

I. HELP RESIDENTS GET BACK MORE THAN THEIR DEPOSITS

How can you end your rental relationships on a positive note—and generate more profits doing so? It's to your advantage to help vacating residents get their full deposit back *plus* give them financial incentive to cooperate during this transition. Here's what to do.

First, give residents a checklist reminder of how the property must be returned to you with the goal of receiving their full deposit back. This checklist should have clear, simple, but specific instructions so vacating residents don't have to make guesses about what you expect.

Offering thank-you and referral bonuses helps me fill vacancies before they exist. That's why I need their cooperation. First, I ask if I may start to show the house two to four weeks before they move out. Knowing they'll receive a bonus, they're more likely to cooperate when I show prospects the property. They're often willing to help show it for me and

---

The Reason Behind the Checklist

Why wait until residents have left to tell them specifically what you needed them to do? Tell them the full details while they have an opportunity to make the situation right. Let them know in advance you're giving them the checklist because you sincerely want them to receive their full deposit. And offer a bonus—beyond their full deposit back. I offer a $50 "transition" bonus as a thank-you for their cooperation during the transition. As noted previously, I also offer bonus money for finding qualified residents to move before their last day.

Even Deadbeats Want a Little Money!

Even individuals you're evicting would like some "transition" money, wouldn't they? I make the same offer to them. Some landlords question me on this, arguing, "Jeffrey, why would you give money to somebody who already owes you several hundred dollars?"

I answer that I make the offer because I want to cut my losses and let residents leave on a positive note, even those I'm evicting. If I don't, that several hundred dollars owed in back rent may become several thousand.

"How's that?"

If the residents I'm evicting are upset, they may play hardball and drag out the eviction procedure as long as they can. In some states, they can tie up the property for extra months before the sheriff has to be called to remove their possessions. All the while, I have no rental income.

Plus, out of spite, the evicted residents may do all sorts of damage, even destroy the property, before finally moving. Why would I want someone who's leaving my property upset with me? I've got too much to lose—not just thousands but tens of thousands of dollars in damage that they could do.

You bet, I'll give them $50 or $100 cash after they've moved out on an agreed date and I've checked that no damage has been done. First and foremost, I'm focused on getting my property back on the market as soon as possible.

Although you want all rental relationships to end on a positive note, sometimes residents simply won't follow your rules. Using strategies in this guide to develop the right kind of relationship with your residents should at least foster a noncombative ending. If residents fail to follow the rules and noncompliance occurs, continue to take action in a business-like way—even when going through an eviction. Never appear angry or out of control in the presence of your residents; simply go through the steps required by law. Be polite in your communication and always put notices and requests in writing (no need to have confrontations over the phone or in person). The residents either comply with your rules and the law or they don't. Regard this process as just another part of the business.

even point out positive features. They're also likely to have the place looking in move-in condition for those showings. I can even step into another room and encourage the applicant to talk confidentially with vacating residents about the home or neighborhood. They always find something good to say. Even if a prospective resident stops by unexpectedly, vacating residents are likely to cooperate and share good things about the place.

Steps to Evict Residents

When you must evict residents, keep these actions in mind:

- The first time you seek to terminate a tenancy or do an eviction, I suggest seeking counsel from an experienced landlord colleague or attorney.
- Study state laws, especially the section relating to termination and eviction.
- Make sure you know the exact steps required by your state. Doing even one small thing incorrectly could cause your case to be dismissed and you'd have to start the process over.
- If you're evicting for nonpayment, don't be quick to accept partial payment because that may affect your right to continue eviction.
- If residents comply before the eviction process is completed, be glad that you kept a businesslike approach. You want the relationship to continue as positively as possible.

What's the secret? By treating them as 3-Star Residents and developing a good working relationship during the rental term, I benefit from vacating residents passing on the good will I've established. This happens whether I'm present at the showing or not. And giving a financial incentive doesn't hurt, either. This approach definitely fills the vacancies faster—all because I'm willing to give a $50 bonus, which I *don't* pay unless I get a qualified applicant before the vacating residents' last day of occupancy.

II. LEAVE DOOR OPEN FOR GOOD RENTERS TO RETURN

When good residents leave with their entire security deposit plus a bonus, you leave the door open for possible future connection and assistance. Be sure to keep the names of good residents who move out. Send them a letter by e-mail or snail mail at least once a year. Ask if they're satisfied with their current rental and if they're in the market for a new place. If they're not satisfied or their housing needs have changed, they may consider looking at what you have to offer. (I've had former residents contact me and rent from me a second time years after they first rented from me.) If they're not in the market themselves, encourage them to refer friends, colleagues, or family members.

III. TRANSITION RENTERS INTO HOMEBUYERS

If you've had a win-win relationship with residents throughout the rental term, your relationships (and profits) don't have to end when they want to buy a house. Most real estate investors miss out on a tremendous opportunity to extend their relationships with their residents. Why not make money not only on the front end of the relationship, but on back end of it, too?

Follow me closely with this idea. *The Landlord's Survival Guide* isn't just another book to read and put on the shelf. Pull out this guide at least once every six months and use it every time you have vacancies or get new residents. Refer to it when you need more cash flowing or funds collected. It will give you the specific recommendations you need.

In this final step, I want to share another revolutionary idea—one of the most powerful moneymaking concepts revealed. This concept alone is worth one hundred times the cost of this guide. Are you ready?

1. Help Residents Purchase a Home by Giving Rewards

From surveying my vacating residents, I've discovered that the number one reason they move is because they're buying a house. I thought about this and had a revelation. If residents want to buy a house, they don't need to simply give me a 30-day notice and say good-bye. As a real estate investor, I can find them a house and put together a deal that's better than one they could find on their own.

On top of that, I can help them buy and/or finance their first home plus make additional profits myself. Putting this idea into action allows me to make money at the back end of the rental relationship by helping them transition from being renters to homebuyers. Talk about a win-win relationship!

If you are creative, you can buy properties below market price (find motivated sellers and/or a house that needs work). Then you can prepare the property for sale (ready-to-move-in condition) and offer it to your residents at market price with terms that make it easy for them to pay (e.g., you could include full or partial financing).

"Rent from Us Today; Buy from Us Tomorrow"

Mike Rukavina, a real estate investor friend who is past president of the Stark County Real Estate Investors Association in Ohio, successfully uses this philosophy in his real estate business. He makes money both as a landlord and an investor who buys properties at a discount, rehabs them, and sells them to his residents who become homebuyers.

I love the slogan Mike uses in his business communication with residents starting from day one. I think it helps them correctly view the desired rental relationship. It is: "Rent from us today; buy from us tomorrow. Choose from one of our rental units now, and as your situation changes, we'll help you move into the home of your choice."

Wow. That's how I'd like residents to regard a "normal" kind of relationship between landlord and resident/buyer. Become a strong believer in what Mike calls the Jeffrey Taylor philosophy that once you get customers, keep offering them more, meet all their needs, and make more money.

In this scenario, your residents win because they purchase a nice home they may not have been able to own as quickly without your help. You win because you realize additional profits in various ways. (For example, you could make money from the profit margin over what you paid for the house. Perhaps you'd make money from any spread you create with financing terms you offer the resident above what you're paying. If you're making underlying payments on a mortgage of $800 a month while the resident pays you $1,000 a month, you're making a monthly profit of $200 for *X* number of years. Or the resident could get a first mortgage and you carry back a second mortgage for the equity you created.) The payments you receive for the next several years become profit. And you feel good about helping people you know as dependable residents become homeowners.

The kind of relationship in which your renters transition into buyers requires changing the way residents see the landlord-tenant relationship between you and them. You want the change in their perception of the relationship to begin as early as possible—ideally when a prospective resident first comes in contact with what you offer.

The goal is clear: to get residents to see you as someone who can meet *all* of their housing-related needs, far more than four walls and a floor. The point is that by meeting housing needs of your customers, you can add value, increase customer satisfaction and retention, plus boost your cash flow. This idea simply extends that philosophy.

Be sure to inform your 3-Star Residents that you offer a Future Homebuyers program. I ask this magic question (which is also on my application): Would you like to buy a home within the next two to three years? If you rent one of our homes, we'll help you buy your first house. That sounds good to prospective residents; owning a home is the American Dream, after all.

In our Future Homebuyers program, we explain that we provide credit in the form of $100 vouchers every month residents pay on time—vouchers given by us, not money that was theirs. Those vouchers can be used toward the purchase of a home that we help them buy. That sounds great to prospective residents. Surely no other landlord has made them that offer. I've just given myself a unique and competitive advantage over all other rental owners in the area.

As part of the Future Homebuyers program, we inspect the property every six months. Every time the resident passes inspection, we add another $100 voucher to the growing total. Whose money did I say is represented by the vouchers? Not theirs. Mine. From a legal standpoint, I don't want residents to think that money is being credited from the rent they are giving. None of the rent they give each month has anything to do with the vouchers accumulated. There is no equitable interest being built up. The vouchers are gifts that aren't awarded until residents fulfill the requirements of the program.

What if residents don't pass an inspection or pay late? Then the value of all previous vouchers becomes null and void, and they start again accumulating voucher credit toward purchasing a home. I believe in being fair and creating win-win situations, so I address the rules clearly during the new resident orientation. I don't conduct any surprise inspections. Whenever I make an appointment to conduct an inspection, residents receive a reminder a few days before. I give them a checklist that tells them exactly what to do to pass, which they like. This removes any subjectivity on either side. If they follow the list, they know they'll pass the inspection and I've met my goal, which is to get residents to take care of the property. All they had to do to get another $100 voucher was do what they should anyway—pay on time and take care of the property.

2. Give Incentives for Paying On Time

Often the reason some residents don't take care of property is because they have no incentive. They think, "The property isn't mine. Why should I spend extra time on it?" They have no investment at stake.

The Future Homebuyers program gives them an investment that grows $100 each month. Every month, send residents a thank-you voucher that reads: "This is to acknowledge that we received your recent rent payment on or before the due date. As part of the Future Homebuyers program, you are entitled to receive this $100 voucher good toward the purchase of a home. The value of all vouchers received is added into your Future Homebuyers account. Please note that if any rent payment is received after the due date, all vouchers and the total amount accrued up to that point is considered null and void. Therefore, it's important to continue your excellent payment record. Thank you once again for your payment."

As the money accumulates—$800, $900, $1,000—residents start thinking of themselves as homeowners, not renters, and take care of the property. They not only keep paying rent on time; many start paying early!

3. Resident Receives Money at Closing Table

To use the money represented by the accumulated vouchers, give the residents a minimum time requirement to be in the program. For example, a resident must rent the property for at least two years. At the end of two years, I don't just give them money when they want to buy a home. The money represented by the vouchers is credited to the home purchase when we're at the closing table and they're purchasing a home from me. If they're not buying a home from me (or a broker or builder participating in my program), money is not credited.

How do you benefit? During the previous two years, residents have taken care of your property exactly the way you want and paid you on time. Would you consider paying out $2,800 a disadvantage? (The vouchers total $1,400 for the first year—$1,200 for 12 on-time payments, plus $200 for passing two inspections. During the second year, the vouchers again total $1,400.) Are you concerned this money is coming out of your pocket? Remember, my policies are called moneymaking management policies. The $2,800 only comes out of your pocket if residents buy a house from you. If you're selling a home to them, you'll most likely make several thousands of dollars in profit up front and perhaps thousands or tens of thousands more if they make mortgage payments to you. You come out well ahead in this situation.

4. Program Offers Great Flexibility

The Future Homebuyers program is not limited like a lease-option program where the residents only option is to buy the home they are renting. Why use a program with that limitation? The proposed Future Homebuyers program allows for a lot of flexibility for all parties. Under this program, the resident may buy any home that the real estate investor is able to buy or control and that they can come to a mutually acceptable agreement. You may own a multifamily building and not want to sell that property to a resident. No problem; the resident can buy *any* property you can gain, buy, or control. After residents have successfully been in the program for a year, the landlord can approach them and get more specific about the type of home they'd like to buy that will meet their needs. Why would a resident want to leave a relationship in which someone is helping them find and buy a house?

The homebuying selection doesn't have to be limited to a house the real estate investor can buy or control. You could decide to work with a builder or broker in the area with which you've partnered. This gives residents even more choices.

Working with a real estate broker, for example, they might decide to buy one of the homes listed. The broker has already agreed that, if the landlord has a qualified buyer, the broker will credit back up to 2 percent of the sales price at closing from part of the commission.

E*verybody* **W***ins!*

Let's say the residents have gone through the Future Homebuyers program for two years. They choose and qualify to buy a home the broker has listed for $150,000. We're at the closing and the residents want their $2,800 credited at closing. Where does the $2,800 come from? It comes from the broker, not me! The broker covers the cost of the accumulated vouchers. This is a win-win-win deal! The resident has the money credited at closing. The broker sold a house, and only had to rebate part of the commission, less than 2 percent of the sales price and less than a normal payout if he or she had to share a commission when another agent is involved. The landlord didn't have to pay out any money, plus received rent on time for two years and the property had been well cared for.

Note: Depending on the price range of homes in your area, I suggest the fixed amount of money credited monthly into the resident's Future Homebuyers account be less or more than the $100 used in our example. If homes average less than $150,000, the monthly voucher could represent $50 instead of $100, which is still a good deal for the resident/homebuyer.

Not all residents who participate in the Future Homebuyers program qualify to buy a house after two years. On average, only 20 percent do. The other 80 percent keep renting from you because, if they move, they'll lose the money accumulated. Instead of leaving, they continue renting longer to qualify at a future point.

Transitioning residents into buyers is a perfect way to end the rental relationship with your residents and something that will become more common. A few major real estate companies with property management divisions have already started implementing similar arrangements with rental residents.

This well-kept, profit-generating secret is now out the bag. However, it's really just good business sense. It's about meeting the needs of the customers and continuing to profit from the relationship as long as additional needs can be met. No need to lose profits to others if you can continue to meet the needs of your residents.

Do you see that you don't have to limit your role in the relationships you create with your residents? Real estate investing can be fun, especially when residents work *with* you instead of against you. Always end relationships on a positive note. Even if your residents move, they may later refer others to you simply because they still feel good about how the relationship ended, and because you took time to follow up with them after their move.

By using your knowledge to fully serve the needs of your residents and/or their friends' needs, you can make profits on both the front end and the back end of any rental relationship. Just remember, having a good relationship with your customers can extend far beyond the first anniversary date. When you continue it for a long time, if not a lifetime, you can double or triple your real estate profits.

Now you can see *even more* why I encourage you to end your relationships on a profitable note!

FINAL CHALLENGE AND GUARANTEE FROM MR. LANDLORD

While speaking at a seminar recently in Connecticut, I recognized an attendee who subscribes to my *Mr. Landlord* newsletter and has even joined me on one of our fabulous annual Landlord Getaway Cruises. After sharing one particular moneymaking management concept, I asked him if he'd used it, saying it could easily add $1,000 per rental to his annual cash flow. Even though he'd read about this concept in my newsletter and heard me teach it three times, he hadn't taken one simple step to implement the idea. I flat out asked him, "Why not?" His honest response was, "Procrastination."

I want to offer "straight talk" to you as your landlording coach. I'm convinced you didn't borrow or buy this guide just to have something else to read. We all take in so much useless information daily, it's easy to become numb and inactive when we come across information that can greatly benefit us! So, don't treat this guide like the newspaper you read quickly then toss off. Take heed and take notes right in the margins of this book; it will help you increase your bottom line.

Sometimes I feel like reaching out to my readers and gently shaking them so they'll stop sleepwalking through their rental business. I urge you to *stop* going through the motions by reading publications and attending seminars but continuing to run your business the "same old way" month after month, year after year.

GET SERIOUS NOW

It's now time to *get serious* about boosting your wealth by following these moneymaking management success steps you've learned in this book:

Step 1—Develop the Right Mindset

Step 2—Identify Your Landlording Success Team

Step 3—Study What You Must Know to Survive

Step 4—Fill a Vacancy with the Ideal Resident

Step 5—Screen Out Problem Residents

Step 6—Conduct a New Resident Orientation

Step 7—Get Your Money

Step 8—Maximize Your Cash Flow

Step 9—Keep Residents Long After Their First Anniversary

Step 10—End All Relationships on a "Profitable" Note

Don't miss out on greater real estate profits and cash flow by going through the motions of reading another book. I'll say it again: *That's not why you originally picked up this guide.* You want greater success; this guide will help you obtain it.

I suggest you go back and highlight portions of what you read, then test and incorporate the strategies *immediately!* You will see positive results. And if you don't, send back this guide directly to me at Box 64442, Virginia Beach, VA 23467. I will personally buy the book back from you. How's that for a guarantee!

Because I am confident that this guide will help you achieve positive results, I invite you (once you have implemented one or more of the ideas in this guide and experienced positive results) to send your success story directly to me at the preceding address. I'm now in the process of gathering 100 landlording interviews and success stories from real estate investors who have read my book, and, as a result, have improved their cash flow. I will share many of these stories in an upcoming follow-up to this book. Those who contribute stories that are published will receive a free autographed copy of the book with a personal word of thanks.

ESSENTIAL RENTAL FORMS

Rental Application/Future Homebuyer

Separate application required from each applicant age 18 or older. Credit check fee of $_____ for each application.

Today's date: _____

Occupancy date desired: _____

Rental price range: _____

Type/size desired: _____

Rental address shown: _____

How did you find out about this property? _____

Applicant's Personal Information

First name: _____ Middle: ___ Last: _____

Any other names you've used in the past:_____

Driver's license/ID number/state: _____

Social Security #: _____

Cell phone: _____

E-mail address: _____

Additional occupants: (List every occupant's name below and their relationship to applicant.)

_____

_____

Residence History

Present street address: _____

City: _____ State: _____ Zip: _____

Dates lived at this address: _____

Own ____ Rent ____ Occupy ____

Current phone: _____

How many pets did you have? _____

Type of pets: _____

Name of present landlord/manager: _____

Landlord's phone: _____ Monthly rent: _____

Are you paid in full? _____

Reason for moving: _____

_____

Have you given notice that you're moving? _____

Number of late payments in past year? _____

Deposit amount currently held by landlord? _____

What is one feature or amenity that you like at your current home? _____

Previous residence address:_____

Previous landlord: _____

Previous landlord's phone: _____

Dates lived at this residence: _____

Reason for moving: _____

Was your full security deposit returned? _____

Number of late payments: _____ Monthly rent: _____

Income history: _____

Applicant's current employment status:

Full-time _____ Part-time (less than 32 hrs/wk) _____

Student _____ Retired _____ Self-employed _____ Unemployed _____ Other _____

Primary source of employment: _____

Average weekly hours: _____

How long at this place of employment? _____

Address: _____

City:_____ State: _____ Zip: _____

Phone: _____ Position: _____

Supervisor: _____

Please indicate weekly, biweekly, monthly average take-home pay: _____

Additional or previous employment: _____

Average weekly hours: _____ How long at this place of employment? _____

City:_____ State: _____ Zip: _____

Phone: _____ Position: _____

Supervisor: _____

Please indicate weekly, biweekly, monthly average take-home pay: _____

Additional Income

If there is an additional, verifiable source of income you'd like considered for qualification, please list income source and requested information below regarding each source (e.g., child support, Section 8 voucher, etc.).

Additional Source

Amount: $_____ per _____

Contact person: _____

Phone: _____

How long have you been receiving income from this source? _____

In the event of some emergency that would prevent you from paying rent, is there a relative, person, or agency that could assist you with rent?
Emergency contact: _____

Phone: _____ Relationship: _____

Assets/Credits/Loans
Note: Only cars on application are authorized to be on premises.

Number of vehicles: _____ Make/model/color/year: _____

Plate #(s): _____ State: _____

Financed/leased through: _____

Monthly payment: _____

Credit Card or Loan (e.g., bank, finance company, department store, gas card, or student loan)

Creditor: _____

Phone: _____ Acct. #: _____

Total amount owed: _____ Monthly payment: _____

Are your payments current? _____

List approximate amounts of any other current monthly expenses:

Cable/Satellite TV: _____ Medical payment: _____

Health insurance: _____ Auto insurance: _____

Tuition: _____ Renter's insurance: _____

Child care: _____ Other: _____

Amount: _____

Bank Reference

Name of bank and branch: _____

City: _____

Checking or savings account #: _____

Number of years account active: (C): _____(S): _____

Average monthly balance: (C): _____ (S): _____

Personal/Professional References

Personal reference or name of nearest living relative: _____

City: _____ State: _____ Zip: _____

Relationship: _____ How long: _____

Phone: _____

Name of doctor: _____

Phone: _____

City: _____ State: _____ Zip: _____

Professional reference (e.g., attorney): _____

Phone:_____

City: _____ State: _____ Zip: _____

Preferred method of "worry-free" standard rental payments:

Electronic banking: _____ Payroll deduction: _____

Charge card: _____ Debit card: _____

Other method of payment requiring additional $_____ handling fee:

Check _____ Money order _____

Preferred type of rental desired:

Standard _____ Custom home _____ Deluxe _____

Preferred rental due date:

Old-fashioned plan (monthly) _____ or Payday plan (biweekly) _____

How long do you plan on living in the next rental home that meets your needs? _____

Would you like to receive a rental gift on your anniversary date as part of a 3-Star Resident Program? _____

Would you like to buy a home within the next 2–3 years? Yes _____ No _____

Do you smoke? Yes _____ No _____

Check the following items you currently own:

Liquid-filled furniture _____ Plunger _____ Lawn Mower _____

Appliances (if so, which ones): _____

Have you ever:

Broken a lease? _____

Refused to pay rent for any reason? _____

Been evicted or asked to leave a rental unit? _____

Filed for bankruptcy? _____

Been convicted of a crime? _____

Will you give us permission to do a criminal background check? _____

Is there anything to prevent you from placing utilities in your name? _____

Do you know of anything or any reason that may interrupt your ability to pay rent? _____

Free Upgrade Bonus/Referral Reward

Final note: Our company offers a free upgrade or referral reward for residents who recommend anyone to us who decides to rent a separate unit from us. Please give the name and phone number of a friend, relative, or co-worker who may be interested in renting. We will contact that person to inquire about applying for and renting one of our other homes or apartments.

Name: _____

Phone: _____

THANK YOU!

Thank you for completing an application to rent from us. Please sign below. Please note that a completed application requires submission of the following, which will be copied and attached to this application:

_____ Driver's license or sheriff's picture ID. Note: Rentals will not be shown without picture ID

_____ Personal check (to verify bank)

_____ Two weeks of most current pay stubs or other proof of each income source listed

Agreement and Authorization

The credit check fee is charged on all rental applicants for the purpose of verifying the information furnished on this application. By signing below, applicant hereby represents all information on this application is true and complete, and hereby authorizes a credit check to be made, annual verification of information, and communication with any and all names/references listed on this application for continual rental consideration or for collection purposes should that become necessary. This fee is refundable/nonrefundable/or applied to applicant's move-in costs if accepted.

Applicant acknowledges this application will become part of the lease agreement, if approved. If any information is later found to be incorrect or misleading, this will be sufficient reason for immediate eviction and loss of security deposit.

Applicant's signature: _____

Date: _____

Sample Notice of Denial for Housing

FROM: _____

Date: _____

Re: Your application to rent the property located at the following address:

_____

This notice is to inform you that after careful consideration, your request for housing has been denied because of the item checked below:

❏ Application incomplete or unable to verify all information provided.

❏ You did not meet the minimum requirements for acceptance at this time, though the decision was not made based on information provided on your credit report.

❏ Negative or adverse information found on the credit report provided by the following:

(If the third box is checked above, the following line includes the name and telephone number of the consumer credit reporting agency providing the credit report; including a toll-free number if this is a national credit reporting agency.)

_____

_____

In addition, if box three is checked above, the consumer credit reporting agency above did not make the decision not to rent to you and cannot explain why your tenancy was denied. The agency only provided information about your credit history.

This notice is provided to meet the requirements of the Federal Fair Credit Reporting Act. You have the right under this act to obtain a free copy of your credit report from the consumer credit reporting agency named above, if you request it within 60 days of this notice. You also have the right to dispute the accuracy or completeness of your credit report and add your own consumer statement (up to 100 words) to the report.

For more information, contact the above-named consumer credit reporting agency.

We also invite you to check back with us in case we can help with your housing needs in the future.

Owner/Manager: _____

Date: _____

Sample Rental Agreement

1. Parties: This agreement is entered into on this date _____, between the following parties, RESIDENT(S):

_____

_____

and OWNER/MANAGER:_____ .

Resident(s) agree to rent from the Owner the premises at the following location subject to the terms and conditions of this Agreement.

Rental Home Address

2. Move-in Costs: _____

Amount charge/description: _____

_____

Rent: $ _____Monthly or Biweekly rent (circle one)

Security Deposit: $ _____Refundable deposit per Agreement

Additional Deposit: $ _____See attached addendums

Other: _____

Total Due: _____

3. Custom Home: The Resident(s) agree to rent from the Owner(s) the premises located at the above address and the home includes the following furnishings, amenities, and upgrades:

_____

_____

_____

4. 3-Star Resident(s): The rental term will begin on _____ and continue on a month-to-month basis. Either party may terminate the tenancy or ask to upgrade the terms by giving the other party _____ days' written notice. As part of our 3-Star Resident Program, we, the Owners and Managers, look forward to serving Residents' housing and related needs for the next three years until the following date _____. During the next three years, Resident(s) will receive property upgrades as Resident(s) in good rental standing. As part of the 3-Star program, the following upgrade (part of your Custom Home rental package) will become your property after the _____ year of the rental term. Because this item will become Residents' property, Resident(s) agree to be responsible for maintenance and/or repair of the item(s).

5. Payday Rent Payment Option: Resident(s) have the option to pay a monthly (the old-fashioned way) rent of $_____ payable in advance on or before the first day of each month. Or, if Resident(s) prefer and consider it more convenient, they may pay a biweekly (every two weeks to coincide with paychecks) rent of $_____, payable in advance on or before _____ of every other week. Resident(s) choose the Monthly Plan or Payday Plan (circle one). If Payday Plan is selected, please note that this becomes a biweekly arrangement, not a monthly.

6. Standard Worry-Free Payment Methods: Resident(s) may select one of the following standard "worry-free" payment methods for paying rent during the rental term, so they don't have to worry about late charges every month. Resident(s) agree to give authorization for rent collection by the method selected and debit appropriate account(s).

Preferred method of payment selected:

❏ Electronic debit from checking/savings account:

❏ Debit card or credit card debit from following account:

❏ Payroll deduction sent directly from employer or debited directly in owner's account.

Payment may be made by traditional methods, such as check or money order, and requires an additional handling fee of $_____ per transaction. Please make checks payable to: _____

Check or money order should be delivered to following address:

_____

7. Due date/late payment charge: Regular payments are due by the _____. Resident(s) agree that if rent is not received by 5:00 PM on the due date, Resident(s) shall pay a late payment charge of _____.
Be advised that any payments lost in the mail or any dishonored checks will be treated as if unpaid until received by Management. Dishonored checks will also be subject to an additional fee of $_____, and must be made good by cash, money order, or certified check within 24 hours of notification. If a check is returned unpaid for whatever reason, checks will no longer be accepted for at least six months. Resident(s) will be required to pay by certified funds only. To avoid potential problems, Resident(s) should select one of the worry-free payment methods.

8. Allocation of payments: All money received from Resident(s) is first applied to any past due balance on Residents' account, including unpaid rent, deposits, damages, or utility charges and any additional charges or fees. Second, the balance of money received is then applied to current rent due.

9. Utilities: Resident(s) further agree to make all utility payments (that they are responsible for) on time during the term of this tenancy. Resident(s) will be considered in breach of this Agreement for any nonpayment, and will be held liable for any resulting added charges and damages. Resident(s) are responsible for the following utility charges: _____

10. Occupants: No more than _____ occupants shall occupy the premises, and only the following listed residents: _____

Persons other than those specifically listed shall be strictly prohibited from staying in the rental unit for more than 7 consecutive days, or a total of _____ days in any 12-month period. For clarification of this stipulation, "staying in the rental" shall include, but not be limited to, long-term or regular houseguest, live-in baby sitters, visiting relatives, etc. Resident(s) shall notify Management in writing any time they expect any guest will be staying in excess of the time limits in this paragraph. Additional residents cannot occupy the premises without first being approved by Management and are subject to full screening procedures. If additional Resident(s) are accepted, acceptance is subject to paying additional rent and security deposit. Unauthorized Resident(s) are a violation of this agreement and are grounds for termination.

11. Assignment and subletting: Resident(s) will not sublet or relet any part of the premises or assign this Agreement without prior consent of the Owner or Manager.

12. Financial hardship: Because unforeseen circumstances may occur during the rental term that may create difficulty for Resident(s) to make timely rent payments, Resident(s) agree to work with Owner and permit direct contact from the Owner with the following individuals, companies, or organizations for assistance in past due rental payments. The following individual has agreed to provide assistance for payment of rent should Resident(s) need temporary financial assistance.

Emergency Contact:

Phone:_____

Charge the following debit/credit card number if rent becomes more than _____ days past due.

Card number: _____

Exp. date: _____

Cardholder's Signature: _____

13. Quiet enjoyment: Resident(s), family, and guests shall not make or allow unreasonable noise or sound. Resident(s) and/or guests shall not disturb other Residents' peaceful enjoyment of the premises. Disorderly conduct will result in a notice to vacate the premises and the termination of Agreement. In addition, Resident(s) are responsible for all actions, conduct, and damages caused by Residents' guests.

14. Major maintenance guarantee: Resident(s) understand and agree that the following major repairs are the responsibility of the Owners and Managers: _____

_____

_____

The Owners and Managers agree to guarantee that these major repairs will be fixed within 72 hours after notification of the problem to Owner/Manager. The Resident(s) understand that if a major repair is not corrected within 72 hours after notification, they will receive FREE RENT on a prorated basis starting the fourth day after the day of notification until the problem is addressed. The maintenance guarantee will not be honored if the maintenance problem was caused because of the Residents' negligence, abuse, or fault. The Resident(s) also agree that in order for the owner to honor the guarantee, the Owner or Manager must be given access into the building, with the Residents' permission, to correct the problem. Free rent will be awarded in the form of a cash rebate following the next on-time rent received.

15. Yard/grounds: Resident(s) shall properly care for and mow the grass and adequately water the lawn, shrubbery, and grounds. If yard is not properly maintained, Management reserves the right to hire someone to mow or care for the yard and charge the expense to Resident(s) as additional rent after first advising the Resident(s) that they have 72 hours to handle the responsibility.

16. Insurance: Owner and Manager are not responsible for any loss or damage to property owned by Resident(s) or guests. It is understood that all Resident(s) should or are required to carry renter's insurance for fire, extended coverage, and liability to cover accidental injury and damage or loss of personal property due to fire or theft or other casualties.

17. Nonwaiver and accepting payments: Should the Owner or Manager accept any partial or late rent payments, this in no way constitutes a waiver by the Owner, nor affects any notice of eviction proceedings previously given. Waiver by either party of strict performance of any provision of this Agreement shall not be a waiver of or prejudice the party's right to require strict performance of the same provision in the future or any other provision.

18. Pets: Resident(s) and/or guests shall not maintain any pets on the premises without prior written consent of the Owner or Manager. Any animal not permitted and discovered on the premises will be considered a stray. All strays will be reported to the proper authority and removed at Residents' expense. No animal, bird, or fish of any kind will be kept on the premises, even temporarily, except properly trained dogs needed by blind, hearing-impaired, or disabled persons, and only under the following circumstances: _____

_____

If a pet is accepted (not referring to trained dogs for assistance), such acceptance is subject to payment of a higher monthly rent and additional deposit. Please refer to Pet Addendum (if applicable).

19. Extended absence: Resident(s) will notify Owner or Manager in advance if Resident(s) will be away from the premises for _____ or more consecutive days. During such absence, Owner may enter the premises at reasonable times to maintain the property and inspect for needed repairs.

20. Disclosures: Resident(s) acknowledge that the Owner or Manager has made the following disclosures:

❏ Disclosure of information on Lead-Based Paint and/or Lead-Based-Paint Hazards

❏ Other disclosure:_____

21. Future Homebuyers Account: Resident(s) understand and agree that following each on-time payment received, the Owner has agreed to provide a $_____ voucher to the Resident(s). During the rental term, the total amount of the vouchers received will be referred to as the Future Homebuyers Account for the Resident(s). Once the Resident(s) have resided in their rental for a minimum of _____ years, the Future Homebuyers Account can be used solely as credit toward the purchase of a house, and that credit is applied or paid out at the time of real estate closing. The house Resident(s) may apply the Future Homebuyers Account toward can be selected from either the same residence in this Agreement or another home offered by the Owner, or from one of the following builders or brokers: _____

Please note: If rent payment is received late, the total money accrued in the Future Homebuyers Account up to that point becomes null and void. The account starts again to accumulate with the next on-time rental payment. Resident(s) further understand and agree that Resident(s) are: (1) responsible for handling all minor repairs and upkeep, and (2) responsible for passing semiannual property inspections. Resident(s) will receive an additional $_____ voucher every six months (following each inspection passed) added toward their Future Homebuyers Account. Two property inspections are conducted yearly with a checklist provided to Resident(s) in advance of inspections. Failure to handle minor repairs and upkeep or failure to pass a property inspection nullifies the total amount accumulated up to that point in the Residents' Future Homebuyers Account.

22. Use of premises: The premises shall be used as a dwelling unit and for residential purposes only. Resident(s) shall use, in a reasonable manner, all facilities, utilities, and appliances on the premises and shall maintain the premises and facilities in a clean and sanitary condition at all times, and upon termination of the tenancy shall surrender the premises in as good condition as when received, ordinary wear and tear and damage by the elements excepted.

23. Plumbing: Expense or damage caused by stoppage of drains and waste pipes, overflow of bathtubs, toilets, or washbasins caused by Residents' conduct shall be Residents' responsibility to repair.

24. Alterations: Resident(s) shall not make any alterations (including painting, nail holes, contact paper, or wallpaper) to the premises without Manager's or Owner's prior written consent. All curtains, miniblinds, fixtures, shelves, and carpet present in the premises before move-in must remain when Resident(s) vacate. In addition, locks may not be changed or added without Owner's or Manager's prior written permission. And if permission is granted for new keys, a copy of any new keys will be given to the Management within three days after the change. If Resident(s) are locked out of the premises, there is a charge of $_____ to open the premises between the hours of _____ and a charge of $_____ for opening the premises beyond those hours. Additional charges apply if key is lost and locks must be changed.

25. Vehicles: Only authorized vehicles may be parked on the premises. These vehicles include: _____. All vehicles kept on the premises must be operational and have current registration, tags, decals, and licenses required by local and state laws. Any vehicle not meeting these requirements or unauthorized vehicles will be removed at the Residents' expense after being given 72 hours notification. Vehicles must be parked only on designated areas. Resident(s) understand that no repairing, servicing, or painting of vehicles is permitted on the premises. Resident(s) also agree not to park or store a recreational vehicle, motor home, or trailer of any type.

26. Notification of problems: The Resident(s) agree to report any roof leaks or plumbing, electrical, heating, or air-conditioning problem or to immediately report any property defect that the Owner is responsible for and could cause possible injury to the Resident(s) or further damage to the property. Failure to notify the Owner or Manager makes the Resident(s) liable for damage to the property resulting from slow or non-notification of the problem.

27. Free upgrade renewal: The Owner agrees to offer a free property upgrade to any Resident(s) who recommend and refer someone to one of our rentals, and that person is accepted and moves in.

28. Security deposit: The security deposit is to be applied to remedy any default by Resident(s) in performance of Residents' obligations under the lease and to repair damages to the premises caused by Resident(s), not including ordinary wear and tear. Within _____ days after delivery of possession of the leased premises to back to the Owner or Manager, the deposit shall be refunded to Resident(s) or an accounting of deposit expenditures shall be given to Resident(s). If costs or repairing damages exceed the amount of the deposit, Resident(s) shall be responsible for all such excess costs. Resident(s) may not at any time apply the deposit to be used as last month's rent or for any other sum due under this agreement.

29. Appliances: Unless otherwise stated as part of the custom rental package, this rental agreement does NOT include any appliances. Appliances that are located on the premises may be sold to the Resident(s) or removed at Owner's expense. While awaiting removal from the premises, Resident(s) are free to use them; however, Resident(s) do so at their own risk. In the event appliances fail to function, the Owner is not liable for repair or damages.

30. Assigned manager: The following person is designated by the Management Company to manage the premises. This same person is designated to receive receipt for all notices and requests upon the Management Company at the following business address: _____

The best time for the Resident(s) to reach the Manager for business-related matters is during the following days/times: _____

The phone number to call is _____

For emergencies, outside of business hours, call _____

31. Access of premises: Owner or Manager shall have the right to enter the premises in order to inspect premises, schedule necessary or agreed repairs or improvements, supply necessary or agreed-on services, or show the premises to prospective residents, purchasers, or contractors. Except in case of emergency, agreement to the contrary by Resident(s), or unless it is impractical to do so, Owner or Manager shall give Resident(s) at least 24 hours' notice of intent to enter, and may enter only at reasonable times. Resident(s) shall not unreasonably withhold consent to enter the premises.

32. Build creditworthiness: A review of Residents' performance is done and placed in Residents' file every year. The Owner or Manager will provide Resident(s) with a copy of GOOD performance reports when so earned. Good reports are earned by residents who pay on time and follow ALL terms of the rental agreement. Resident(s) can then give copies of the reports to future landlords, loan officers, banks, and mortgage companies. These reports may be beneficial in helping Resident(s) rent or buy a car or house in the future. Building credit may also help Resident(s) participating in the Future Homebuyers Program. Similarly, nonpayment of rent and any judgments are reported to all three major credit bureaus, and violations of any rental terms are put into Resident's file, and will be made available to future landlords, banks, and other creditors who Resident(s) may want to do business with in the future. Therefore, it is important that Resident(s) understand that the credit they establish through performance reports during the rental term (good or bad) can affect their credit for many years. Because of such importance of performances reported, Resident(s) will always be notified when a nonpayment or rental violation occurs, and the Resident(s) will be given an opportunity to immediately correct any rental violation before it is put in Resident's file or reported to the credit bureaus.

33. Lease violation: If Resident(s) violate any provision in this Agreement, that violation is grounds for termination, and Owner or Manager has the right to begin eviction procedures with appropriate notice and procedures allowed by law.

34. Satisfactory inspection: Resident(s) have personally inspected the premises and find them satisfactory at the time of execution of this agreement unless as noted on the Property Condition Checklist. Resident(s) further acknowledge that the premises are equipped with a smoke detector that was operating at time of inspection. Resident(s) agree to periodically test the smoke detector, replace the battery as needed, and inform the Owner or Manager immediately of any malfunction.

35. Additional provisions to this agreement: Unless noted, no other provisions or promises have been made to Resident(s) except as contained in this Agreement. Any additions or modifications to this Agreement must be in writing. Additional promises or provisions that are part of this Agreement are listed as follows:

_____

36. Joint liability: Each person signing this Agreement as a Resident is jointly and severally liable for all the terms of this Agreement.

37. Read this entire agreement: That Resident(s) acknowledge that they have read all the stipulations contained in this rental Agreement, and the Owner or Manager has answered all questions and discussed the Agreement with them. Resident(s) agree to comply and have received a copy of this Agreement.

Resident's signature: _____

Date: _____

Resident's signature: _____

Date: _____

Owner/Manager/Agent signature: _____

Date: _____

Sample Cosigner Agreement

This agreement is between Resident(s) _____,

_____

Owner/Manager and cosigner(s) _____

This agreement is entered into on the following date: _____,

and forms part of the rental agreement between Resident(s) and owner listed above for the leased premises at the following address: _____.

The cosigner has completed a separate rental application for the purpose of permitting the Owner/Manager to check the cosigner's creditworthiness, including running a credit report.

Though the cosigner has no intention of occupying the leased premises, which would/wouldn't be a violation of the rental agreement, the cosigner agrees to be liable (if Resident(s) do not pay in a timely manner) for any of the Residents' financial obligations of the rental agreement. Those obligations include but are not limited to: unpaid rent, property damage, cleaning and repair charges, and legal fees that exceed the Residents' security deposit.

Though the owner has no legal obligation to report to the cosigner, any nonpayment of financial obligation by the Resident(s), both the Resident(s) and the cosigner understand that the owner reserves to right to send notices to the cosigner of the Residents' failure to meet any financial obligations of the rental agreement. Prompt payment by the cosigner who receives notice of pending legal action may help to avoid additional legal or court costs.

If any legal proceedings arise out of the rental agreement, the prevailing party shall recover reasonable attorney fees, court costs, and reasonable fees necessary to collect a judgment. Hopefully, with the assistance of the cosigner, these added expenses will not be necessary.

Resident signature: _____

Date _____

Cosigner signature: _____

Date _____

Owner signature: _____

Date _____

Sample Property Condition Checklist

Dear _____

Address _____

Welcome to your new residence. We thank you for choosing to rent from us. Please check off each of the following areas of the rental unit to confirm with us that each area is in satisfactory condition prior to your moving in. Any additional notes to this list must be submitted to the management within 3 days of the date of this checklist. Thank you for your cooperation. (For large homes, attach a second page to this checklist.)

	Satisfactory			Satisfactory	
	Yes	No		Yes	No
Entrance door	_____	_____	Bedroom #1	_____	_____
knocker/bell	_____	_____	ceiling	_____	_____
peephole	_____	_____	walls	_____	_____
deadbolt lock	_____	_____	floors	_____	_____
Living room	_____	_____	windows	_____	_____
ceiling	_____	_____	screen	_____	_____
walls	_____	_____	elec. fixtures	_____	_____
floors	_____	_____	Bedroom #2	_____	_____
windows	_____	_____	ceiling	_____	_____
screen	_____	_____	walls	_____	_____
elec. fixtures	_____	_____	floors	_____	_____
Din Rm or Bedroom #3			windows	_____	_____
ceiling	_____	_____	screen	_____	_____
walls	_____	_____	elec. fixtures	_____	_____
floors	_____	_____	Bathroom		
windows	_____	_____	ceiling	_____	_____
screen	_____	_____	walls	_____	_____
elec. fixtures	_____	_____	floors	_____	_____
Kitchen			windows	_____	_____
stove	_____	_____	screen	_____	_____
refrigerator	_____	_____	elec. fixtures	_____	_____
cabinets	_____	_____	medicine cab.	_____	_____
sink	_____	_____	mirror	_____	_____
counter tops	_____	_____	tub	_____	_____
ceiling	_____	_____	sink	_____	_____
walls	_____	_____	shower	_____	_____
floors	_____	_____	General		
windows	_____	_____	porch/balcony	_____	_____
screen	_____	_____	heating system	_____	_____
elec. fixtures	_____	_____	water heater	_____	_____
General			front yard	_____	_____
back door	_____	_____	back yard	_____	_____
mail box	_____	_____	garage/driveway	_____	_____

Special Remarks (cleaning or repairs needed) _____
_____

We hereby acknowledge that we have inspected the above mentioned rental unit and have found everything to be in satisfactory condition except as stated otherwise. We understand that we are liable for any new damages that may occur during our occupancy.

Resident(s) _____ Date _____

Mr. Landlord's Mini-Glossary

The following terms have a unique meaning within the context of this text and as communicated by the author when giving Mr. Landlord trainings.

anniversary date   Once a resident has resided in the property for a year, that date is considered the resident's anniversary date. This date should not be referred to as the "end" of rental term or the renewal date, which could give residents the impression that if they're thinking about moving, now is a good time. Instead, the word *anniversary* implies a time to celebrate a "continuing" relationship.

automatic payment plan   Rent is paid automatically to the landlord without the need for resident involvement (e.g., automatic electronic debit from checking account or payroll deduction).

custom home   One level up from a standard home in which a property has been customized with one or more property upgrades to meet the needs or desires of residents.

deluxe home   The highest level of home customization in which several upgrades have been selected by residents and added to the home.

Future Homebuyer   A term a landlord uses to convey an expectancy to residents that he or she is making provisions to assist them in buying a house.

headache history   A screening criterion that evaluates the history of the applicant regarding headaches he/she has given to previous landlords and the likelihood of creating headaches for future landlords.

hope factor   The degree to which a landlord does nothing purposely to improve the odds of success but simply hopes things will turn out the way they want.

lifetime resident value   Total amount of income a landlord can receive from each resident over the time the resident is a customer. It reflects both direct and indirect income the landlord receives by customers referred by the resident.

maintenance guarantee   A policy reassuring residents that the landlords will handle their obligations in a timely manner. It allows residents to remain patient—and not contact housing authorities—if the landlord doesn't immediately respond to property concerns. Residents know they'll get free rent if the delay continues.

payday payment plan   Setting up rent due dates to coincide with a resident's paycheck schedule.

people-centered management Management makes decisions that take into account feedback received from residents and/or incorporates policies that allows both parties to benefit.

preventive communication Communication in which certain issues or rental terms are addressed with residents to prevent problems regarding those issues.

property manager The preferred title a landlord uses when describing his or her "role" to residents instead of *owner.*

referral reward A bonus (e.g., free property upgrade) given to individuals who refer a qualified resident who moves into a property.

standard home A basic, average home with four walls, a ceiling, and a floor.

supersize it To add one or more upgrades to a standard rental home. This increases the value to a custom "combo" package for which residents willingly pay additional rent.

target marketing Marketing that reaches prospective residents most likely to want the property instead of just anyone who breathes. It offers features and attracts prospects who qualify, cause fewer problems, and stay long term.

3-Star Residents Term used to emphasize to residents that the landlord appreciates, respects, and rewards them for being long-term customers.

VIP Resident A promotion in status for 3-Star Residents that entitles them to additional perks after residing in the same rental for three years.

worry-free payment method A method for delivering rent money on time to the landlord through an automatic payment plan without residents having to remember to mail checks and possibly be late. It helps them to avoid late charges and eviction proceedings, and jeopardizing the tenancy.

The following books and Web sites can assist new or part-time real estate investors in finding additional information on effectively managing rental property. Most of these books are available for sale on the "Books" section of the MrLandlord.com Web site.

Books

The Landlord's Kit by Jeffrey Taylor, Dearborn Trade Publishing.

This book of forms is the companion to the guide you're reading. It includes over 150 sample rental forms, letters, and checklists for communicating to residents in every rental situation.

Landlording by Leigh Robinson, Express Publishing.

The Unofficial Guide to Managing Rental Property by Melissa Prandi, MPM, Wiley Publishing.

Every Landlord's Legal Guide by Marcia Stewart, Ralph Warner, and Janet Portman, Nolo Press.

The Goldmine of Brilliant Tax Strategies by Albert Aiello, Home Rental Publishing.

Secrets of a Millionaire Landlord by Robert Shemin, Dearborn Trade Publishing.

Wealth Protection Secrets of a Millionaire Real Estate Investor by William Bronchick, Dearborn Trade Publishing.

The Complete Idiot's Guide to Making Money with Rental Properties, Second Edition by Brian and Casey Edwards, Alpha Books.

Down to Earth Landlording, A Guide to Successful Part-time Property Management by Don Beck, Skyward Publishing Company.

Increasing Occupancy by Mindy Williams, Rent & Retain Systems (especially helpful for apartment owners).

Property Management for Dummies by Robert Griswold, Wiley Publishing.

How to Collect the Money You Won by Jim Martin, Judgment Enforcement Center.

Web sites

http://www.mrlandlord.com

At this official Web site of the author, you can find all the keys to your success as a rental property owner, including state-specific rental forms, landlord-tenant laws for all 50 states, management software, and the most-visited Internet forum for questions and answers regarding problems with rental property and residents.

http://www.tenantcreditchecks.com

Provides low-cost tenant credit reports on prospective residents and reports debts of former residents to all three major credit bureaus.

https://www.clearnow.com

Assists landlords in setting up automatic rent payments or direct rent deposits with residents. *Mention this guide when you contact them and they will let you try this service free for three months.*

http://www.usdoj.gov/crt/housing/title8.htm

Visit to view and print the Fair Housing Act.

http://www.hud.gov/offices/lead/outreach/leapame.pdf

Visit to view and print the pamphlet titled, "Protect Your Family From Lead in the Home." Landlords are required to give copies of this pamphlet to residents of pre-1978 built properties.

http://www.hud.gov/offices/lead/1018/lesr_eng.pdf

Visit to view and print the lead disclosure form.

http://www.ftc.gov/os/statutes/fcra.htm

Visit to view and print the complete Fair Credit Reporting Act.

http://www.phada.org/linkha.htm

Link to local housing authority Web sites nationwide.

http://www.narpm.org

Site for National Association for Residential Property Managers (for finding property managers specializing in assisting owners of single-family rentals).

http://www.realestateassociations.com

Visit for a nationwide directory of rental owner and real estate investor associations.

Special Free Offer for Buyers of This Guide!
Receive a Free MrLandlord.com Take Control Kit

As my way of saying thanks for buying this guide, I'd be glad to send you the free MrLandlord.com Take Control Kit ($100 value). But I'd like to ask one small favor. Please tell your real estate friends about this resource and the MrLandlord.com Web site. You will receive all of the following as part of the Take Control Kit:

- Free six-month subscription to our rental owner newsletter
- Three *free* special reports (guaranteed to add to your success as a real estate investor). These reports cover the following topics:
  - Over 80 sources of money to buy or renovate properties
  - How landlords can limit their liability (protect their assets)
  - Real estate checklist of 200 possible tax deductions
- One *free* tenant credit report
- Three *free* months of unlimited direct rent deposit service
- One *free* audio CD with a management training section by Jeffrey Taylor, the author

To request your free Take Control Kit, call toll-free 800-950-2250, 24 hours a day. Or, you can fill out this form, copy it, and mail it to Mr. Landlord, Box 64442, Virginia Beach, VA 23467. Or, you can fax this request form to 757-436-2608. There is a $5.95 charge for shipping and handling, including fax requests. Privacy policy: None of your information will be sold to another party.

_____ Yes! Send me the free Take Control Kit that includes all of the above, including the free six-month rental owner newsletter featuring news of additional free items and services that will help me take control and with my real estate investments. You can charge my credit card below to cover shipping and handling.

Please Print Clearly

My name: _____

Phone: _____

Address: _____

City: _____ State: _____ Zip: _____

Credit card #: _____

Exp. date: _____

Visa _____ MC _____ Amex _____ Discover _____

Signature: _____

Date requested: _____

Total: $ 5.95 for shipping and handling. Check enclosed _____

How many units do you own? _____

How many years have you been a real estate investor? _____

E-mail address: _____

Thanks for letting us be part of your real estate success team!

Special Half-Price Offer for Buyers of This Book!
MrLandlord.com Rental Forms Software

MrLandlord.com Rental Forms Word Processor CD Software. Now that you are ready to take action and start implementing the moneymaking action steps recommended in this guide, we suggest that you get the CD program that includes all the forms you will need (and more) in an easy-to-use word processing program. It's available for a limited time to buyers of this book for *half* the regular price. This CD will allow you to edit, personalize, and print 150 recommended rental forms and letters, including all those referred to in this *Landlord Survival Guide* and almost every other rental form you will need.

Here are just some of the many forms you will receive:

Application and Verification Forms

Custom Home Packages—Popular Upgrades
Follow-Up to Inquiry
Holding Deposit Disclosure
New Resident Checklist
Rental Application
Pet Application
Consent to Perform Checks
Questions for Former Landlord
Legal Reasons for Nonacceptance
Denial Based on Credit Report
Plus 16 more . . .

Leasing Forms and Addendum Forms

Sample Rental Agreement
Property Condition Checklist
Payday Payment Plan
Automatic Rent Authorization
Pet Agreement
Garage/Storage Rental

EPA Lead Pamphlet
Lead Disclosure
Future Homebuyer Program and Sample Voucher
Plus 20 more . . .

Collection and Violation Notices

Rent Statements/Sample Invoices
Late Fee/Returned Check Notice
Excessive Utility Violation
Noise Violation
Automobile Violation
Pet Violation
Good Tenant Letter
Warning to Report Residents
Letter to Emergency Contact
Notice of Debt Forgiveness
Plus 21 more . . .

Maintenance/Management Forms

Introduction of New Management
Maintenance Guarantee
Notice of Intent to Enter

Independent Contractor Agreement
Mold Addendum
Resident Release of Recreational Items
Smoke Detector
Reward for Reporting Crime
Agreement with Property Manager
Plus 24 more . . .

Retention/Turnover/Marketing Forms

Updated/Verification Resident Information
Holiday Gift Certificate
3-Star Resident Letter
Notice of Rent Increase
Exit Survey
Itemization Security Deposit Returned
Resident's Referral Reward Policy
Marketing Letter to Neighbors
Marketing Letter to Colleges
Marketing Letter to Local Businesses
Plus 24 more . . .

There are over 100 additional forms not listed. You can print any of the recommended forms in minutes and produce professional-looking forms for your residents anytime. To order this Forms CD software, call toll-free, 800-950-2250, 24 hours a day. Or you can fill out this form, copy it, and mail to Mr. Landlord, Box 64442, Virginia Beach, VA 23467.

_____ Yes! I want the Rental Forms CD with 150 forms (regularly $99) for the special *half-price offer* of only $49.50, plus $5.00 shipping.

Please Print Clearly

My name: _____

Address: _____

City: _____ State: _____ Zip: _____

Credit card #: _____

Exp. date: _____

Visa _____ MC _____ Amex _____ Discover _____

Signature: _____

Date ordered: _____ Total: $ _____

Check enclosed: _____ Phone: _____

E-mail address: _____

You may also fax your request by calling 757-436-2608, 24 hours a day. Free shipping for fax orders, save $5.00.

Jeffrey Taylor, known as Mr. Landlord, is the nation's number one landlording coach for real estate investors who want to make money with rental properties.

Author of the best-selling book *The Landlord's Kit* (featuring more than 150 forms), he teaches and communicates with more rental property owners in America than any other landlording expert. His column, "Mr. Landlord on Management," is syndicated in over 100 real estate association newsletters. He has published the most-read real estate newsletter, *Mr. Landlord*, for two decades. With more than 75 million hits since 1999, Taylor's Web site MrLandlord.com currently averages 1 million page views a month. Widely sought as a real estate expert by the media, he has appeared multiple times on CNN.

Taylor served as a trainer for a property management firm before starting his own management consulting company. Through it, he has conducted nearly 1,000 workshops teaching people-centered, practical, and proven moneymaking management strategies. In addition to his formal real estate training, he's learned from the "school of hard knocks," as both he and his wife, Dot, have owned and managed residential properties from single-family homes to apartment buildings for 23+ years. He's also learned from teaching and exchanging ideas with hundreds of investors.

Taylor is a frequently requested speaker for real estate investor, rental property, and apartment associations. If you'd like to know when Jeffrey Taylor will be speaking in your area, call his office at 757-436-2606. Also call this number to invite Jeffrey to speak to your real estate association at a monthly meeting, conference, or convention.